BIBLE DELIGHT:

*Heartbeat
of the
Word of God*

For the busy, sometime burdened, Christian worker, ever giving out, here is proper nourishment for the soul. I suggest a section a day! For me it is marvellously real and refreshing.

Dick Lucas
Formerly Rector of St Helen's Bishopsgate, London

BIBLE DELIGHT:

*Heartbeat
of the
Word of God*

*Psalm 119 for the
Bible teacher
and Bible hearer*

Christopher Ash

2008

PTMEDIA

CHRISTIAN
FOCUS

Scripture quotations marked ESV are taken from *The Holy Bible, English Standard Version*, copyright © 2001 by Crossway Bibles, a division of Good News Publishers. Used by permission. All rights reserved.

Scripture quotations marked NIV are taken from the Holy Bible, *New International Version*. Copyright © 1973, 1978, 1984 by International Bible Society.Used by permission of Hodder & Stoughton Publishers, A member of the Hodder Headline Group. All rights reserved. NIV is a registered trademark of International Bible Society. UK trademark number 1448790.

Scripture quotations marked NRSV are taken from the *New Revised Standard Version Bible*: Anglicized Edition, copyright 1989, 1995, Division of Christian Education of the National Council of the Churches of Christ in the United States of America. Used by permission. All rights reserved.

ISBN 978-1-5271-0803-5

Published in 2008
Reprinted in 2011, 2019 and 2021
by
Christian Focus Publications,
Geanies House, Fearn, Ross-shire,
IV20 1TW, Scotland, Great Britain
www.christianfocus.com
with
Proclamation Trust Media,
Willcox House, 140-148 Borough High Street,
London, SE1 1LB, England, Great Britain.
www.proctrust.org.uk

Cover design by Moose77.com
Printed by Bell & Bain, Glasgow

Contents

Dedication

To John and Katie, Andy, Barnaby and Lizzie

Note on Translation

The translation used in this book is similar to other reasonably close versions such as the NRSV and the ESV, but with two important differences. First, I have tried so far as I can to be consistent in translating the main Hebrew words by the same English word. Second, I have attempted (sometimes at the expense of elegance) to show as many as possible of the structural and stylistic features of the poem, for example when verses begin or end with the same word.

In some verses, as elsewhere in the Psalms, we are not sure what English tense best translates the Hebrew. This is a notoriously difficult issue in translating Hebrew poetry, and I am not competent to adjudicate; I have generally followed the NRSV or ESV.

Series Preface

This is the first in a series of books which looks at the culture and context of preaching and teaching God's Word. We need help not just in 'how to preach Bible books', but clarity on the point and purpose of preaching and teaching. The books in this series will be short and accessible, ideal for personal use, group study or for training. The following titles are planned:

Bible Delight: Heartbeat of the Word of God
The Practical Preacher (revised and updated)
Preaching that Builds the Church
Training Preachers: What it takes to make a preacher
The Lifelong Preacher: Keeping fresh, keeping focused

Christopher Ash's book, *Bible Delight: Heartbeat of the Word of God* is an excellent foundation for the series. It gets us to the heart of our motivation to read, preach and teach. In his own words: 'we preach out of Bible delight in our own hearts and for Bible delight in our hearers' souls.' Christopher's Bible material is Psalm 119 – the great psalm of Bible delight!

The introductory chapter focuses our minds on the essence of Bible delight. The 'meat of the book' then works systematically through the text of Psalm 119, taking each of the twenty-two sections in turn. Additional material ('Getting our Bearings in Psalm 119') is included in the chapters dealing with the first two sections. Personal response questions are included at the end of each chapter.

While the primary purpose of the book is to stimulate Bible delight in teachers and hearers of God's Word, the book would be an ideal guide to tackling a preaching or teaching series on Psalm 119.

David Jackman and Robin Sydserff
Series Editors, London, March 2008

Acknowledgements

I am grateful to those who have given me opportunities to preach this wonderful psalm, first at the Evangelical Ministry Assembly and the St.Helen's City Partnership Summer School in 2006, and subsequently at the Cornhill Training Course and in various churches. My thanks also to my colleagues at The Proclamation Trust both for their encouragement and for their own modelling of Bible delight in their lives and ministries. These thanks are especially due to Robin Sydserff and David Jackman, the Series Editors, and to Zoë Moore for her painstaking proof reading and editorial work.

Christopher Ash
March 2008

Introduction

The Essence of Bible Delight

Oh, how I love your instruction!
All the day it is my meditation.
(Ps. 119:97)

The purpose of this book is to stimulate Bible delight among Bible teachers and Bible hearers. Specifically, my aim is to persuade those of us who teach and preach the Bible that we can only do so faithfully when we ourselves are thrilled with what we teach, and further that our aim ought to be to stimulate the same delight in our hearers. That is to say, we preach out of Bible delight in our own hearts and for Bible delight in our hearers' souls. To put it negatively, if we preach out of what Dr. Martyn Lloyd-Jones used to call 'ossified orthodoxy', then we will breed that same ossified orthodoxy in our hearers.

If someone asks you or me, 'Do you love the Bible?' we might reply - if we are Christians - 'Well, I know that I ought to love it. But to be honest I am not sure that I do. My Bible reading is more a matter of duty than delight. I wish it were a delight, but all too often it is a chore.' If so, Psalm 119 is for you. If you are not a Christian believer, that may sound a stupid question. 'Of course not,' you may respond. Perhaps you love the Bible as literature. But I am not talking about loving the Bible as literature. I am talking about loving the Bible for its substance. If you want to know why Christians love the Bible, you cannot do better than to start with Psalm 119.

It is especially for you if, like me, you have a high view of the Bible. We are persuaded that the Bible is trustworthy. We believe it is the word of God himself. Perhaps we are happy to speak of it as 'inspired', even 'infallible' or 'inerrant'. And yet even for us, until and unless we love the Bible and find it a delight, our view of the Bible is too low. There are hints in the psalm that the singer was what we would call a Bible teacher. For example, in verse 79 he prays that 'those who fear' God will 'turn' to him in order to 'know your testimonies'. It is unsurprising that one who could compose this remarkable psalm would be employed in teaching the word of God. If so, it is a challenging example of the heart of Bible delight that ought to beat in our own Bible teaching.

On the common where we used to walk our dog there is a golf course. Beside one fairway we came across one of those benches donated in memory of someone. I forget the name of this man, so let us call him Fred. The bench simply read, 'To Fred, who loved his golf.' I was a little sad that this was the best they could think to say about Fred. But presumably he did love his golf. And I imagine they knew he loved his golf because he played it so much. What he played showed what he loved. His sport was his delight.

If I were to ask you, 'Do you play with your Bible?' you might be surprised, even offended. 'No,' you might say, 'the Bible is much too serious to play with.' But there is another way of looking at it. As the legendary Liverpool football manager Bill Shankly famously said, 'Some people believe football is a matter of life and death. I'm very disappointed with that attitude. I can assure you it is much, much more important than that.' And, joking apart, what we play may not be trivial at all. After all, they knew that Isaac was married to Rebekah because he was seen playing or sporting with her in a way that only made sense if she was his delight (Gen. 26:8, 9).

Introduction

As we read and pray through Psalm 119 we keep company with one who delighted in his Bible. Bible delight is the heartbeat of this psalm. We might even say that he plays with Bible words, as he turns from one word to another in an elaborate poetic playfulness. More than twenty-five times he says he delights in the word of God, or loves and longs for the word of God. To him it is delicious (v. 103) and delightful. As he reads it he keeps stumbling across treasure (v. 162). It is his hope, his peace, his joy, his song, his freedom and his comfort.

He had much less of the Bible than we do. Certainly he had no New Testament. Probably he didn't have all our Old Testament. We don't know who wrote the psalm, or when. But he loved his shorter Bible. From his psalm we may learn the logic and the dynamics of Bible delight. I pray that as we learn to sing his psalm, we too may learn to love our complete and even richer Bibles, and that our hearts will beat in time with his, the heartbeat of Bible delight.

CHRISTIAN EXPERIENCE AND THE PSALMS

Before we launch in to Psalm 119, let us take a step back from Bible delight to think about Christian experience more generally. What does it *feel* like to be a believer? When someone asks, 'How are you?' what do you say? Most of us reply, if we are below a certain age, 'I'm good, thanks' (although as a cultural dinosaur I think it would be more correct to say, 'I'm well, thanks!'). But sometimes I feel like the girl in a recent mobile 'phone advertisement. She is on her mobile, and a friend asks, 'How are things with Mike?' Her face crumples and she replies, 'How long have you got?' (and how glad she is of her free minutes). 'How are you?' 'How long have you got?' In any group of Christians, that kind of honesty would unlock a flood of Christian experience told as it actually is, and not as we would like to pretend it is.

What does the Christian life feel like? What ought it to feel like? What is authentic Christian experience? This question is important for assurance, lest we worry that our experience shows we are not Christian at all. It is important for our expectations, so that we do not give up when the going gets tough. It is important for evangelism, so that we tell people honestly the life into which we invite them. It is important for stability, otherwise we are always worrying that we are missing out, that if only we read this book, or went on that course, or attended the other conference, or somehow got ourselves to where the latest wind of doctrine was blowing, well, then we would feel alright at last. So it is an important question: what does the Christian life feel like?

One of the great functions of the Psalms is to shape our ragged emotions and desires, so that we not only think as we ought to think, but also feel as we ought to feel and long as we ought to long. If we are familiar with the doctrine of Total Depravity we will know that this important doctrine does not teach that we are all as bad as we could possibly be; that would be absurd and make it impossible to account for self-sacrifice, virtue, honesty, kindness, and goodness in all sorts of people. The doctrine of Total Depravity means that every part and facet of our human personhood is touched and tainted by sin, including our desires and feelings. When we moved into one house my wife bought two wooden flower tubs. They had been made by sawing an old whisky barrel in two. She asked me to drill drainage holes in them. And as I bored into the wood with my bit and brace, there was an unmistakable whiff of whisky. The whisky had seeped into every fibre of the wood. Wherever you drilled, you would find it. In the same way human sin has seeped into every fibre of human personhood. Our minds, our hearts, our feelings, our bodies, our desires, all alike are impregnated with sin. And this includes our feelings: we do not feel as we ought to feel. Sometimes we are happy at others' misfortune, or sad at their success. We do not want what we ought to want; our loves are disordered. We love what we ought to hate, and we shun what we ought to desire.

Introduction

The Psalms give us authorised, authentic response to God and his word. We learn in them not only what he has said to us (the word of God coming down); we learn also how we may and ought to respond (the word of God going back up). The Psalms are therefore of great practical importance in the Christian life, and a vital protection against imbalance. In past ages, those who called themselves 'evangelical' were derided as 'enthusiasts' (e.g. by Mgr. Ronald Knox in his famous book *Enthusiasm*); we were thought to be too emotional at the expense of the intellect. Now it is the reverse. Since the advent of the charismatic movement in the 1960's some of us may look askance at some of the excesses of that movement. We want to say to our charismatic friends (in love!), 'You are too focused on experience, and therefore you are not stable, you follow every new fad, you are not breeding maturity, you are characterized by superficiality.' But in response they may say to us (also in love!), 'We may be too focused on experience. But to listen to some of you preach and speak, it does not seem to us that you have any emotions at all, or any real experience of the living God!'

Too often this conversation is a dialogue of the deaf. I want to suggest that a thoughtful, sensitive, and theological restoration of the Psalms into Christian prayer and praise may provide God's way forward. For the Psalms perfectly combine thought and feeling, theology and prayer, emotion and reality, the subjective and the objective. In particular, Psalm 119 can inject into the heartbeat of Christian experience the passionate and reasonable delight in the written word of God.

LEARNING TO SING THIS PSALM (HOW TO USE THIS BOOK)

I have been challenged by this description of one seventeenth-century minister who preached 190 sermons on Psalm 119. A contemporary wrote that he 'writes like one that knew the singer's heart, and felt in his own the sanctifying power of what he wrote.' His sermons began with the understanding, dealt with the affections, but drove purposefully towards the promotion of practical holiness. 'They come to the conscience; first presenting us a mirror, in which we may view the spots of our souls, and then directing us to that fountain in which we may wash them away.'

This book has the same aim of promoting joyful holiness. It is intended to be a pathway into Psalm 119. The psalm has inexhaustible riches. Every time I come back to it I notice new things. This little book is meant to help us get started in singing it. I hope it may be a helpful first word on the way in; but please don't expect it to be the last.

I take it that my task is more like that of a singing teacher than a biology teacher. A biology teacher can instruct us how to dissect. But, as has been said, 'we murder to dissect'. And a psalm is not just to be analysed. It is for the music room, not the mortuary. If I am a singing teacher, I need to do three things.

First, I need to instruct so that we understand the lyrics. This will involve understanding key words such as 'steadfast love' in their Old Testament context.

Second, I need to teach the tune (metaphorically) so that we feel it as we sing; we are moved and touched by it as well as instructed by it. For this psalm is thick with emotions. It is not flat, grey, or bland, but full of churnings of strong passion.

And, third, I need to motivate so that not only can we sing it, but we want to sing it from the heart.

My task is therefore didactic (teaching the meaning), affectional (tuning in to the feeling) and volitional (moving the will to join in). Some skip the hard work of understanding and go straight to the feelings. The result is fluff, words sung with gusto but the mind not engaged. Others, however, work hard at understanding but never get as far as singing. I have been guilty of this myself. We study the psalm and work hard at its cognitive content; but we are not moved by it. And so we do not join in.

Introduction

But we must join in. For this psalm opens for us a window into a world where the people of God love the word of God. It invites us not just to look in through the window as into a strange world, but to climb in, to enter this world and live in it, as we too sing the psalm. So, as we read, let us ask ourselves three questions.

Do I understand it (the didactic question)?
Can I feel it (the affectional question)?
Am I willing to sing it (the volitional question)?

Because the psalm is for singing, instead of calling the writer 'the psalmist' (as a commentary would usually do), I am going to call him or her 'the singer' as a reminder to us that they sing in order that we may join in the song.

I suggest you use this book and my literal translation as a guide to walk with you through the psalm, perhaps over a period of 22 days (one day per section), or even 22 weeks (giving longer to meditate on each section). You might want to use it as a guide for a Bible study group or reading group. Whatever you do, guard time for prayerful response to the psalm, not only to understand it but to sing it from the heart. I have given a couple of personal response questions at the end of each chapter to help with this.

1

Getting our Bearings in Psalm 119

Why do we find the psalm so hard to sing?

Psalm 119 is by some way the longest psalm in the Bible. My fascination with it began before I was a Christian. When I was a spotty teenager, I used to stand all too early in the morning in school chapel, with about 650 other teenagers. And an impossibly enthusiastic Director of Music would train us to chant psalms. I know that shows what a dinosaur I am, but it is true. He did a good job, musically. And when we were not too sullen, we sang quite well. But it was the triumph of his enthusiasm over our incomprehension, because we had no idea what they meant, all those statutes and precepts and repetitions. And it was so long. I wondered how it could be so long, and how long chapel would last if the chaplain forgot to tell us only to sing one or two sections; if by mistake we were to sing it all, we should certainly miss Physics, and probably French as well.

After I came to a real Christian faith, my fascination with this psalm continued. As Everest to a climber, so Psalm 119 in the Psalter lures us because it is there. But it puzzled me too. How is it that he delights not just in the word of God in general, but in the law of God in particular? I learned that the law brought knowledge of sin and that the righteousness of God became known apart from law (Rom. 3:20, 21; 7:7). I was taught that the law even provokes us into sin, and that sin springs to life when triggered by law (Rom. 7:7-9). I read that the law was a heavy yoke on the neck of disciples, very hard to bear (Acts 15:10). Altogether the law didn't seem a very good thing. I was not expected to delight in the law, but rather to delight that we are not under law but under grace (Rom. 6:15). In the words of the old hymn,

> The terrors of Law and of God,
> with me can have nothing to do.
> My Saviour's obedience and blood,
> hide all my transgressions from view.

And so I couldn't work out why he loves this law, why it is sweet to his taste, and so on. What is going on? This is a problem for us. And unless we solve this problem, there is no way we shall be able to sing this psalm. The solution is outlined in the chapter headed 'Getting our Bearings (B)' below. And it is important, because we must learn to sing the psalm.

Before we address the theological problem of the law, I want to address two other problems. These concern the kind of psalm that Psalm 119 is, its style and genre. I want to encourage us to sing the psalm as it is written, and not just to adopt 'the nugget strategy' or 'the theme strategy'. Most Christians begin with 'the nugget strategy' in Psalm 119. Here we treat the psalm as a mine for nuggets of spiritual gold. We wander or dig through the psalm until some verse catches our eye. When it does, we extract that verse and put it in our collection of spiritual valuables. Perhaps 'the entrance of your word gives light' (v. 130) or 'your word is a lamp to my feet' (v. 105). They are great nuggets. This strategy is a start. But if we stop with nuggets, we imply that the 'non-nugget' parts might as well be tossed into the scriptural skip.

It is perhaps a step forward to take themes and trace them through the psalm. So, for example, we might consider the

Why do we find the psalm so hard to sing?

theme of suffering and study that. But even with this strategy we seem to imply that God would have done better to inspire a collection of thematic studies rather than the psalm as it is.

I think there are two reasons we are reluctant to learn to sing it as a raw psalm in the form in which we have it. First, we find it repetitive. And second, we find it incoherent. Let us take repetition first. The psalm certainly does repeat. About half a dozen times he prays, 'Teach me your statutes'. Many times he prays, 'Give me life ...' (vv. 17, 25, 37, 40, 50, etc). And there is much other repetition. But why shouldn't there be repetition? We need to repent of impatience, and to remember that one man's repetitiveness is another man's integrity and emphasis.

Besides, it does not repeat in a wooden way. This is not the mind-numbing repetition of a jingle from 'Greensleeves' played by the ice-cream van as it stops outside our house day by day (and it always cuts out in the middle; and it's always the same jingle; and it drives me mad!). Rather this is 'a theme and variations'. And as we sing around the theme, we stay on the same central theme, but we see it from fresh angles. And we find ourselves saying, 'I had never quite seen *that* about the word of God.' So there is a freshness about it. It is a little like walking around a beautiful statue with an expert guide. So our singer points out feature after feature of the word of God to help us appreciate more fully the wonder of the whole. I need this kind of varied repetition to get through my thick skull and soften my hard heart. So let us not worry about repetition. Let us savour the repetition and not resent it. God knows that we need it.

But what about incoherence? We might as well admit that we find it disconnected and therefore hard to study, let alone sing. Like some other psalms (e.g. 25, 34) and four of the poems of Lamentations, it is an acrostic. (Ps. 119 is the most elaborate acrostic in the Old Testament.) Each verse in the first section of eight verses begins with *aleph*, the first letter of the Hebrew alphabet. Each verse in the second section begins with the next letter, *beth*. And so on through all 22 letters of the alphabet.

Bible Delight

It is often supposed that this formal structure acts like a straightjacket inhibiting any coherence of meaning. Just as in a child's alphabet book there is no link of meaning between Bird, Bat, and Bacon, so, we say, each eight-verse section is an unconnected jumble of pious thoughts. And just as there is no logical development from Apple to Bat and then Cat, so between sections the psalm as a whole is disconnected. The psalm, we think, has formal shape at the expense of logical meaning.

But this is a poor argument. We might as well say that a rhyming poem must necessarily be nonsense verse, or that alliterative sermon headings are bound to be forced. But we all know that in the hands of a skilled practitioner a rhyming poem may be deeply coherent, the form working together with the content in an ordered whole. The same may even be true for some alliterative sermon points (though not all!).

The poet who wrote this psalm was a very skilled practitioner. The psalm is full of connections. He is a Hebrew poet, and therefore he loves parallelism. Again and again there are connections between adjacent verses, or between groups of verses in fours (typically the first four and the second four of an eight). Sometimes adjacent sections of eight are linked in topic. And sometimes the final verse of an eightsome acts as a climax or summary of the section. The psalm has all the marks of a fruitful and ordered mind.

More significantly, Christian experience does not run in straight lines. No matter how logical we may be, we do not experience God as the stages of a mathematical proof. A psalm that never went round and round and back again might be easier to analyse; but it would be very hard to sing from a real human heart. So let us go with the flow of the psalm, respect its genre, and sing it as it is written.

I make no claim that the particular themes I have identified in each section are all that is there. The psalm contains inexhaustible riches. But I hope that I have made at least a passable case for identifying the themes that I have discerned. I hope

Why do we find the psalm so hard to sing?

my comments may at least help get you started on your own studies.

While these obstacles of structure and form are real, they are dwarfed by the puzzle of substance with which we began. How can we, who are Christian believers under the New Covenant, be expected to sing this psalm of delight in the Old Covenant Law of God? I believe that the first two sections of the psalm address this puzzle. We shall consider the first section (vv. 1-8) and then consider the theological puzzle of the Law as we lead into the second section (vv. 9-16).

Section 1:
Walk the Way of the Word
(vv. 1-8)

Aleph

¹Blessed are those whose way is blameless,
     who walk in the *instruction* of the Lord!
²Blessed are those who keep his *testimonies*,
     who seek him with their whole heart,
³yes, who do no wrong,
     but in his ways they walk!
⁴You have commanded your *precepts*
     to be kept deeply!

⁵Oh that they may be firmly fixed, my ways
     in keeping your *statutes*!
⁶Then I shall not be put to shame,
     having my eyes fixed on all your *commandments*.
⁷I will praise you with an upright heart,
     when I learn your righteous *judgments*.
⁸I will keep your *statutes*;
     do not forsake me deeply!

This first section divides four and four. This shape is signalled
by the final word of verse 4 being the same as the final word of
verse 8. This Hebrew word means something like 'completely'
or 'very much'; I have translated it 'deeply' (or 'deep') here and

23

in verses 107, 138, 140, 167 to try to convey its sense. It is translated 'utterly' in verses 43, 51, and 'exceedingly' in verse 96.

A. THE ONLY WAY OF BLESSING IS TO WALK THE WAY OF THE WORD (vv. 1-4).

Verses 1-4 state the great objective foundation truth upon which the whole psalm is built. Both verse 1 and verse 2 begin 'Blessed are those who(se) ...' Here at the start is a great billboard: Come this way for blessing! There is only one kind of human being who will be blessed. And the challenge to us is this: the man or woman who is blessed is not the one who rests in a *status*, but the one who walks in a *way*. Right at the start of our psalm we need to recapture a manner of thinking about the Christian life that we have neglected. If we asked many Christians how blessing comes, their first answer would not be to describe a walk. 'Blessing', they might say, 'comes through an assured status. I am justified by faith. I know that sin's penalty is paid. I am confident that the righteous anger of God has been poured out on Jesus Christ who died as my substitute (a propitiatory sacrifice). And now I have in my pocket a sure ticket that will give me access through the pearly gates when I die. That is blessing.'

That is gloriously true. But if we stop there it is a truncated truth because we have here a way (1a), a walk (1b), a keeping (2a), a seeking (2b), a doing (3a) and a walking again (3b).

In verse 4 he tells the LORD, 'You have commanded your precepts to be kept deeply!'

He says this, not because the LORD did not know ('LORD, I thought you might like to know that ...,' or '...just in case you had forgotten'), but to show that he, the singer, has begun to grasp this great truth. He has begun to understand that this is the only way to blessing, to walk the way of the LORD with diligence and integrity.

Walk the Way of the Word (vv. 1-8)

These words 'walk', 'ways' and 'keep' (that is, guard), crop up again and again. The governing metaphor of the life of faith in this psalm is to walk in the way of the LORD. We are to think not just of a ticket, but of a journey. And we will not be able to sing this psalm unless we are persuaded of this gateway truth.

We need therefore to ask who can sing the psalm. Because we might read in verse 1 the words, 'Blessed are those whose way is *blameless*', and respond, 'Well, there we are, I knew I couldn't be expected to sing it! Only one man has ever been blameless, and it is not me. The Lord Jesus Christ can sing this psalm. But he must sing it alone. I always suspected it was a solo and not a congregational piece.'

But this is not so. We do not know who originally wrote and sang this psalm. It is sometimes called 'an orphan psalm' because it has no heading. There are hints that the singer may be a leader and teacher of the people of God. In verse 74 God-fearers see his hope and rejoice. And in verse 79 they turn to him for teaching and example. Perhaps he is a priest or prophet. In some ways this singer is a foreshadowing of Christ (the technical word is a 'type' of Christ), a leader whose career is fulfilled in the Lord Jesus Christ. It has been suggested that the placing of Psalm 119 (about the word of God) next to Psalm 118 (about God's King, the Messiah) is deliberate, the idea being to support the teaching of Deuteronomy 17:18-20 and Joshua 1:7, 8 that the leader of the people of God is to be a lover of the word of God who himself walks the way of the word.

This makes a lot of sense, and it must be right in some ways to see this psalm fulfilled in the Lord Jesus Christ. And yet this psalm is not sung in its entirety by the perfect king, or teacher, or priest. For this singer has gone astray (vv. 67, 176). He is penitent and not perfect. Further, to be blameless does not mean to be sinless. Job was blameless (Job 1:1, 8; 2:3), but he was not sinless. Zechariah and Elizabeth, the parents of John the Baptist, 'walked blamelessly in all the commandments and statutes of the Lord' (Luke 1:6, in a striking echo of Psalm 119);

but they were not sinless. To be blameless is to have integrity, to be the same on the inside as we appear on the outside. (So L. C. Allen translates verse 1, 'How fortunate are those whose way is marked by *integrity*.') It is (v. 2) to have a whole heart and not to be like the Roman god Janus, with two faces. Blamelessness is about direction rather than achievement.

It is striking to note that the Bible can speak of sinners actually keeping the law of God. I have had to revise my understanding of this. I had always taken it as read that no human being could keep the law. And yet, in Genesis 26:5 we read that, 'Abraham obeyed my voice and kept my charge, my commandments, my statutes and my laws.' And yet he was clearly not sinless. And in 1 Kings 3:14 Solomon is told that his father David walked in God's ways, 'keeping my statutes and my commandments', which is, on the face of it, an extraordinary thing to write in the obituary of a man who committed adultery and was complicit in murder. What does it mean? It can only mean that they were believers, that they went where the law pointed, to repentance and faith in the Christ to come. And therefore they knew in anticipation the blessing of justification by faith, of having righteousness accounted to them (cf. Rom. 4:1-8). The same must be true of our singer here.

But the fact remains that there is no alternative pathway to blessing than this wholehearted direction of life. We must walk this walk. And the logic is simple in verse 2. If we are to seek him, we must walk where he walks. The way of the word is the way of the LORD. It is the way he walks. And therefore if I am to walk with him, I must walk this way. If two people agree to go on a walking holiday together, and then one says he is going to the Rockies, while the other insists in walking the Cairngorms in Scotland, it does not take a travel agent to conclude that they will not walk together.

This truth of the absolute need for holiness of life needs to be re-emphasized today. The life of discipleship is not a spectator sport. We do not just watch Jesus walk the walk and then thank God that because Jesus has done it we do not need to. Discipleship is to walk in his ways, to walk the way he walked (1 John 2:6), to walk in a manner worthy of the calling to which we have been called (Eph. 4:1), and to walk in love (Eph. 5:2).

But how are we to respond to this great truth? For this truth is still true under the New Covenant. There has never been, and there will never be, any other way of blessing than walking the way of the word. This is not a redundant truth; it is an eternal truth. Verses 5-8 give us the appropriate response.

B. The Longings of the heart. I need to long to walk the way of the LORD (vv. 5-8).

It is worth noticing that verses 1-3 are the only significant section of the psalm that is not addressed directly to the LORD. In verse 4 the singer begins to respond to the truth of verses 1-3. And from here to verse 176 he stays in prayer. Apart from the occasional aside (such as v. 115) all the rest is 'You, LORD'. He moves from doctrine to prayer; we need to do the same.

And especially we need to encourage those of us who are 'professionals' in Christian leadership to make a habit of this transition. Some years ago John Stott used to give a word of exhortation to Langham scholars, pastors from majority world countries who came here to study theology, and usually to work for a doctorate. At the start of their studies he would say to them, 'There is a real danger that a scholar may return home after three or four years an academic success but a spiritual failure, a 'doctor' (qualified to teach) but no longer a 'disciple'; possessing a new degree and a new title but no new vision, power or holiness...' He used to quote the German theologian and pastor Helmut Thielicke who warned against 'the worst and most widespread ministers' disease', to turn from speaking to God in the second person to merely speaking about him in the third person. This psalm encourages us all to move from the third person (vv. 1-3) to the second person (vv. 4-176), from truth to adoration, from doctrine to prayer.

And it is passionate prayer. We need to feel the urgency in verses 5-8. He longs not to be put to shame (v. 6), an important theme in the psalm (cf. vv. 31, 46, 78, 80). He hopes that on the last day he will not be exposed as a fraud, as one who professed the name of God but did not have his nature, as a child of promise by name but a child of slavery by nature (Gal. 4). He knows that only if the LORD answers his call and changes his heart will this be possible, and he will not be put to shame. Only then will he be vindicated by his Redeemer, justified by his Judge, acknowledged by the Son of Man, and seen to be a son or daughter of God. Only then will he not be ashamed. Only then, as Calvin says, will he have no regrets. And he knows (v. 6b) that for this to be, he must look resolutely ahead with his eyes fixed on walking the way of God's commandments. He longs for this.

He can only praise from an upright heart (v. 7), that is, a heart without hypocrisy, when he learns God's righteous judgments. Learning in this psalm is always practical. He does not just need to learn what the commandments *are*; he needs to learn to *do* them, to keep them by the grace and help of the God who answers his prayer. Only when he gets that help will he be able to keep the statutes (v. 8a). And so he prays desperately for it, 'Do not forsake me deeply!' 'I understand (v. 4) that you have commanded a heartfelt deep keeping of your word; and I understand that unless you give me a heart to do that you must deeply forsake me. There are only two ways to walk, the way of deep Law-keeping and the way of deep God-forsakenness.' And he trembles at that thought. 'He trembles lest he should be left to himself' (Spurgeon).

Verses 5-8 are a real challenge for us to sing. We need to learn to echo this deep longing for holiness. For myself, I think I have sometimes been so concerned to avoid the shallow error of perfectionist teaching (which teaches that perfect holiness is attainable as an achievement in this age), that I have sometimes failed to preach to myself the urgent need and longing for holiness. We need first to understand the truth of verse 4, that only deep holiness of heart will bring blessing. And we then need to avoid the shallow response of cheap grace, which says, 'This is a very high standard. And frankly it's a bit too tough. And so I shall just thank God that Jesus kept the standard for me, so that I no longer need to.' This is not true. We need to sing verse 5 in a fuzzy world and a complacent church: 'Oh that they may be firmly fixed, my ways in keeping your statutes!' 'Lord, make me like that.'

But how? How is this possible? That is the subject of the next section (vv. 9-16).

PERSONAL RESPONSE QUESTIONS

1. Do you believe that verses 1-3 are true? Can you confidently sing verse 4? How do both the world and the church say to us that this is too absolute, and that real life does not divide so simply into two ways to walk?

2. Can you pray verses 5-8 from the heart? If not, what desire or fear prevents you longing for this wholehearted walk? Pause to cast yourself on the grace and mercy of God and let him move your heart to pledge yourself to wholehearted devotion.

2

Getting our Bearings in Psalm 119

Remember the music of grace!

In the first section we sang the objective truth that there are only two ways to walk (vv. 1-3). On the one hand there is the wholehearted walk in the way of the word, which is the way of the LORD; and this is the way of blessing. The only alternative is to be God-forsaken. Either I keep his word deeply (v. 4) or he must forsake me deeply (v. 8). And so I am to long deeply that I may walk his way (vv. 5-8). But how? This is the question with which section 2 begins in verse 9: 'How can a young man keep his path pure?' How can this be possible? The answer to this question is the key to singing the whole psalm with joy and confidence.

But first, why a 'young man'? Why does he sing, 'How can a *young man* keep his path pure?' I first read this as a young man and thought to myself, 'Ah, I know what this psalm is about; it must be about sex!' Calvin suggests that it is a young man because youth is especially the place of decision, the place where two paths meet, the place where big choices are made, and the place where passions rage. That may be so. It is true that Proverbs 1:4 speaks (using the same word) of giving 'knowledge and discretion to the youth'.

But I think Derek Kidner is closer to the mark when he suggests that he writes 'young man' because he himself is that young man. His answer applies just as well to middle-aged women, and anybody else for that matter. He is, as Kidner says, not preaching but praying. He is asking, 'Lord, how can *I* keep my path pure? How can *I* be this one who walks the way of blessing? Jesus does not sing this psalm alone. But how can I sing it with him?' This is the prayer of the individual singer (which NRSV loses by translating it with the gender neutral plural, 'young people').

The theological question is, how can I keep my path pure? The answer to this is the key to singing the psalm. Unless we grasp the answer, this psalm will remain locked away without the music. We can study it, but we will not sing it. This is what some commentators do, when they refer learnedly to 'Torah piety'. Isn't it interesting, they imply, that in those days they related to God like that? Isn't this an intriguing museum piece? And so they seal the psalm into a separate compartment in their Biblical Theology box and make it unsingable by us.

Alternatively, they do some interpretative footwork. For example, one commentator writes, 'A Christian, who is liberated from the yoke of the Mosaic Law, can feast on this psalm by using a simple device ...' His 'device' is to forget what it actually says and, whenever it says 'law' or 'testimonies' and so on, substitute 'love, as described in 1 Corinthians 13.' 'Beyond that,' he writes, 'the Christian must not exert his mind too much as he prays this psalm.' That strategy is to the study of interpretation what I myself am to Scottish Country Dancing: clumpy and uncoordinated.

THE EIGHT 'WORD' WORDS

Throughout the psalm there are eight 'word' words. These are shown in italics in the translation. I have translated these as follows, and put next to them the translations usually used by the

Remember the Music of Grace!

NIV and the ESV. (A number of these words occur in Psalms 1 and 19, which contain similar themes to Psalm 119.)

1. Instruction (e.g. v. 1) NIV Law ESV Law

This is the most common of the eight words, occurring in verse 1 and 25 times in all. It is the Hebrew word *torah*. It comes from the verb for teaching and is a comprehensive term for all words that give direction from God. Often this word is used to refer to the first five books of the Bible, the Torah of Moses. But it can include prophetic oracles (for example, in Isaiah 1:10 it is used of the prophet's words). The word 'instruction' helps to convey this broad sense of the word better than 'law', which we tend to associate with something just restrictive and negative.

2. Testimonies (e.g. v. 2) NIV Statutes ESV Testimonies

This is the Hebrew word *edoth* and conveys the idea of a word that bears witness to the faithfulness of the LORD and at the same time bears witness against the person who breaks faith with the LORD.

3. Precepts (e.g. v. 4) NIV Precepts ESV Precepts

This is the Hebrew word *piqqudim* and means words appointed or charged by someone with authority.

4. Statutes (e.g. v. 5) NIV Decrees ESV Statutes

This is the Hebrew word *chuqqim* and emphasizes the binding force and permanence of what is spoken.

5. Commandments (e.g. v. 6) NIV Commands ESV Commandments

The Hebrew word *mitswoth* refers to the straight authority of the LORD to give orders and expect them to be obeyed.

6. Judgments (e.g. v. 7) NIV Laws ESV Rules

Both ESV and NIV struggle to translate this Hebrew word *mishpatim* consistently, as we shall see below. It refers to the decision, ruling or verdict of a judge. In scripture it means primarily the decisions of God the Judge. But it also means

the judgments we ought to make in response. We ought
to judge as God judges, to make the same decisions. We
ought to 'do his judgments'. (I have commented more on
the translation of this word - see p. 37)

7. Word (e.g. v. 9) NIV Word ESV Word
The very common Hebrew word *dabar* is used in the
prophets in the expression 'the word of the LORD'. It is also
used of the Ten Commandments in Exodus 34:1, 28 and
Deuteronomy 4:13.

8. Promise (e.g. v. 11) NIV Word/Promise ESV Word/Promise(s)
The word *imrah* simply means something spoken. Often in
the Psalms, and especially in Psalm 119, it has the sense of
something promised, which is why I have translated it by
'promise'.

The singer plays with these eight 'word' words throughout the
psalm. Almost every verse contains one of them, although just
occasionally a verse will contain two of them or none. Roughly
speaking, each section of eight verses contains each word once,
although there are plenty of poetic variations. He plays with
these eight words in a kaleidoscopic fashion.

He uses them interchangeably. So, for example, he speaks
equally of *keeping* the precepts (v. 4), the statutes (v. 5), the word
(v. 17), the testimonies (v. 22) or the instruction (v. 44). He
asks to *learn* equally the judgments (v. 7), the commandments
(v. 73) and the statutes (v. 71). And so on. So we are to treat
the variation as freshness of style more than distinctiveness of
meaning.

COVENANT WORDS THAT BEGIN WITH GRACE

For while these eight words may express marginally distinct
facets, they are facets of one central jewel. And this jewel is the
Covenant. Although the word Covenant never appears in the
psalm, it dominates it from verse 1 to verse 176, because these

words are Covenant words. And Covenant is the wallpaper of the psalm; it lies behind every verse.

A study of these words shows that again and again they are used in close connection with the Covenant. 'The LORD' is the Covenant name of God (e.g. Exod. 6:1-7). He gives his instruction, precepts, commandments, statutes and judgments as the written expression of his Covenant with his people.

To take a few from many possible examples: in 2 Kings 17:13, 15, 34-38 the destruction of the northern kingdom of Israel is explained by their rejection of the Covenant, which means not keeping the 'commandments', 'statutes', 'judgments' and 'instruction' of the LORD. (It is also the same as not walking in the ways of the LORD, which links it closely to the language of Psalm 119, e.g. vv. 1-3). In Deuteronomy 33:9 observing the 'promise' is equivalent to keeping the Covenant. In Psalm 25:10 keeping the Covenant is the same as keeping the 'testimonies'. In Psalm 103:18 to keep the Covenant means the same as remembering to do the 'precepts' (the Hebrew word is *piqqudim*, which the ESV curiously translates here as 'commandments'). In Deuteronomy 4:1-13 we see Covenant associated with 'word', 'statutes', 'judgments', 'commandments', and 'instruction'.

When the prophets spoke the word of the LORD, they were preachers of the Covenant.

The strapline of the Covenant is, 'You will be my people and I will be your God.' It is the relationship created and established by the LORD with his people through the redemption out of slavery in Egypt. Because this Covenant is created and established by the LORD through redemption, this means – and this for me has been the most significant breakthrough in enabling me to sing this psalm – that all the eight 'word' words are two-directional words whose first direction is grace. Only under grace do they call us to walk the way of the word.

Our problem is that we read words like 'law' and 'commandments' (and certainly ESV 'rules') to be one-way words. So God speaks from the mountain top of Sinai and says, 'Do this ... and don't do that. Be good boys and girls; and don't be bad boys and girls.' When we think this is what the eight words mean, we have two problems with this psalm. First, when the singer says he keeps them (the commandments etc.), it sounds to us impossibly priggish and self-righteous. How dare he say that? And, second, we cannot make head nor tail of all the times he says he delights in them. It sounds to us like the schoolchild in the playground who goes up to the head teacher with a copy of the school rule book and says, 'Head teacher, I do so love this rule book; would you autograph it for me?' What a creep he seems to us. And so he seems to us to be a priggish creep. This stops us singing the psalm.

By the same token, we cannot understand why it was such a disaster when Moses smashed the two tablets for the Ten Commandments, after the incident of the golden calf (Exod. 32:19; Deut. 9:17). After all, for a head teacher to tear up a rule book in a school assembly would typically be greeted with cheers rather than tears.

But this is to misunderstand the words, which are two-way words whose first direction is grace. They are words that create and sustain relationship. We see this very clearly in Deuteronomy 10:12f, where keeping the 'commandments and statutes' is equivalent to fearing the LORD God, walking in all his ways, loving him, and serving him with a whole heart and soul. To keep the Covenant word is not, and never was, ticking the boxes of a legal checklist. Always it was intended to be a matter of the heart.

It is because these Covenant words create and sustain relationship that it was such a disaster when Moses destroyed them. For the effect was the same as that decreed in Hosea 1:9, that they would be called 'Not my people', and he would not be their God.

It is very important that we are persuaded that these are Covenant words that speak first of grace. Here are three proofs that these words really are grace words.

Remember the Music of Grace!

We have seen that the ESV usually translates *mishpatim* as 'rules'. This is not, I think, a happy translation, as witnessed by the fact that in 6 of its 22 occurrences in this psalm they are forced to translate it differently (vv. 84, 91, 120, 121, 132, 149). The word means the decisions of God the Judge, and it expresses the way he runs the world.

For example, in verse 84b the singer prays, 'When will you pass judgment on those who persecute me?' (and to write 'When will you do rules on those who persecute me?' hardly works as a translation). This judgment is the consistent judicial decision of God in favour of his Covenant people. This is the Just Judge in the parable of Luke 18:7, who will act to vindicate his elect. His judgment is not a rule that we must keep, but rather a decision he makes in our favour if we belong to him.

In verse 132 he prays, 'Turn to me and be gracious to me, as is your judgment with those who love your name.' This word is again the gracious decision of the LORD in favour of his people.

Or again, in verse 149b he prays, 'according to your judgment give me life.' Again, this is not the justice that punishes the deserving sinner, but the judicial decision in favour of the believer.

So this word 'judgments' speaks of the grace of the Covenant God ruling the world in favour of his Covenant people. It speaks not primarily of what we do in response to his grace, but first of what he does in governing the world on behalf of his Covenant people.

PROOF 2: THE SUBSTITUTE 'WORD' WORDS

Four verses of the psalm contain none of the regular eight 'word' words (vv. 3, 37, 90, 122). But each of them seems to have a word that substitutes for the regular eight. These substitutes (shown with a dotted underlining in the translation) help us to understand the meaning of the regular eight. In verses 3, 37, the substitute is the 'ways' of the Lord. The instruction and commandments etc. express not first how we are to walk, but primarily how he walks. They are his ways before they become our ways. They begin with him; that is, they begin with grace.

In verse 90 the substitute word is 'faithfulness': 'Your faithfulness endures to all generations.' And his faithfulness is primarily what he does for us in grace.

Then in verse 122 the substitute word is 'pledge'. 'Give your servant a pledge of good ....' The Covenant word is the solemn pledge of the Lord that he is for us.

So these substitute words are grace words that confirm the grace direction and meaning of the regular eight.

Proof 3: The word 'promise'

The eighth word in my list simply means 'something said'. But the context often indicates that the 'something' is said with the direction of grace. For example, in verse 41 the singer prays, 'Let your steadfast love come to me, O Lord, your salvation according to your promise.' The word 'steadfast love' is the important Hebrew word *chesed* which means a steady unbreakable Covenant love. (We see it most strongly as the refrain in Psalm 136, which recounts the 'wonders' (see on v. 18) of his deeds of creation and redemption. And the 'word' here, the 'promise', is a word that speaks of 'steadfast love' and of 'salvation'. It is a rescue word, not just a word of command from Sinai. And because it is a rescue word, it speaks first not of what I must do for him, but of what he is pledged to do for me.

It speaks of promise; and therefore it speaks of Christ. For in Christ all the promises of God find their 'Yes' (2 Cor. 1:20). As we sing in one song, 'Every promise of our God, finds its Yes in his own Son.' The Covenant is only possible because of the Christ to come. Only in Christ do the Covenant sacrifices for sin have substance. Only in Christ can the Spirit of God be poured out into cleansed human hearts without destroying them.

Remember the Music of Grace!

Whenever in the Old Testament a man or woman believed the promises of God, they believed in the Christ who was to come. When Abraham believed the promise, he believed (in principle) the gospel that was preached to him (Gal. 3:8), and therefore he believed in Christ. When they believed the promises, they believed in the Christ who would fulfil the promises. And therefore this singer is justified by faith in Christ, for there has never been any other way to walk with God. No one can sing this psalm with integrity until and unless he or she has been justified by faith in Christ.

It follows that to try to sing this psalm as if it were a legalistic song, rejoicing in works righteousness, written by a priggish creep, is like setting the lyrics of a lullaby to the music of a punk rock band. It is quite simply the wrong music. For the right music is the music of grace and the melodies of Christ. When we sing it we must tie the law to the promises; we must never divorce the statutes from the Saviour; and we must never cut off the commandments from Christ.

Commenting on verse 103, Calvin asks how we can reconcile the sweetness of the law ('sweeter than honey to my mouth') with the law bringing 'condemnation' in 2 Corinthians 3:9. 'The solution', he writes, 'is easy: the prophet does not speak of the dead letter which kills those who read it, but he comprehends the whole doctrine of the law, the chief part of which is the free Covenant of salvation. When Paul contrasts the law with the gospel, he speaks only of the commandments and threatenings. Now if God were only to command, and to denounce the curse, the whole of his communication would, undoubtedly, be deadly. But ... here the singer affirms that the grace of adoption, which is offered in the law, was sweeter to him than honey.'

THE TEN COMMANDMENTS

Having said this, we need to remember that these eight 'word' words speak both of grace and of response. They begin with grace. But the grace of God trains us to renounce ungodliness (Titus 2:12); it writes the law in our hearts, and moves us to keep it.

The Old Testament law codes (for example in Deuteronomy, or Leviticus, or Exodus 21–23) are all practical outworkings in daily life of the foundation of the law, which is the 'Ten Words' (the Ten Commandments, Exod. 20:1-17). These are 'written with the finger of God' on tablets of stone (Deut. 9:10). That is, as we might say, they are written in very bold type and in a very large font. These ten have a pre-eminent place. All the rest are the outworking of these great commands.

In 2 Chronicles 6:11 we are told that the Ark *contains* the Covenant. And yet the Ark *contains* only the two tablets, the 'Ten Words' (2 Chron. 5:10). So there is a sense in which the Ten Commandments *are* (in compressed form) the Covenant, both grace and response.

So when the singer says that he rejoices in the word of God, he means two things which need to be held together. First and foremost, he rejoices in the Covenant promise of God, that is, in his grace and redemption. But, second, he rejoices in the sheer goodness of the response to which he is called in the Ten Commandments. Let us consider them in turn.

1. Although he lives in a world of many gods (as we do), he is learning to love the LORD his God who redeemed him, and to love no other gods. He is learning to live under the grace of the Redeemer.
2. Although he lives in a world of idols (as we do), he is learning to hate idolatry, the shaping and fashioning of god to be the way he wants god to be.
3. In a world which holds God cheap, he is learning to love the name of God and to care for his honour, and not to cheapen that name by the way he speaks or behaves.
4. In a frenetic and anxious world he is learning to love the Sabbath principle. He has tasted the goodness and sufficiency of God, and will therefore gladly both rest and allow others to rest with him.

5. In a disordered world, he will honour his parents. He understands that this commandment is the tip of the iceberg of honouring those with human authority over us. He submits gladly to this because he submits to the authority of God.

6. In a world full of hate and anger, he is learning to shun any behaviour that harms or desires to harm another human being. He wants now to love his neighbour as himself.

7. In an unfaithful world, he is learning to value sexual faithfulness in the covenant of marriage, and to flee from sexual intimacy in all other contexts. He knows that the universe rests on the Covenant faithfulness of God.

8. In an unjust world, he is learning to hate stealing and unjust business dealings. He is learning to love generosity, to work that he may have something to share and give (Eph. 4:28), because he knows the God who richly gives us all things to enjoy (1 Tim. 6:17).

9. In a deceitful world he hates false witness, lying for our gain and another's harm. He is learning to love truth, because he knows the God whose promises are always 'Yes' in Christ (2 Cor. 1:20).

10. In a self-obsessed world, he is learning to hate greed and covetousness because he is learning to trust the God who has said, 'I will never leave you nor forsake you' (Heb. 13:5).

But in all this, we must take care to put on and keep on the music of grace. The word in which the singer delights is the ✓ Covenant word of God's grace. At no point is the singer self-righteous. Always he casts himself on the mercy and grace of the Covenant God.

THE 'WORD' IS THE BIBLE

Throughout this study, I am going to assume that we may replace any of the eight 'word' words by 'The Bible'. Let me briefly explain why I make this assumption. The eight words are united by the concept of Covenant, that there is one great rescue story of the living God building relationship with human beings.

This one Covenant is fulfilled in Christ. All that comes before Christ foreshadows him. All that comes afterwards speaks of him. He is the principle of coherence of scripture. The Bible is the Father's testimony by the Spirit to the Son. It is one coherent word of Covenant in Christ. This psalm holds together a faith that obeys and an obedience that believes.

In particular, one of the striking features of Psalm 119 is that Law and Gospel are tightly tied together. Luther writes that, '... the prophet looks with spiritual eyes at the law of Moses and sees hidden and enclosed in it the law of faith, the Gospel of grace.'

These words speak simultaneously of his grace to us in the promises, and of our calling to respond with a godly life in keeping the heart and spirit of the Ten Commandments. It will not allow the believer to separate off part of the Bible as 'Law'; for Law belongs with Gospel.

For these reasons, it is right to extrapolate from whatever scriptures the singer had, to the whole Bible that we have. For in essence scripture everywhere speaks of the one Covenant of grace in Christ. What he sang about his (smaller) parts applies even more to the full testimony to Christ that has been entrusted to us.

Section 2:
The Word in the Heart
(vv. 9-16)

Beth

[9]How can a young man keep his path pure?
 By guarding it according to your *word*.
[10]With my whole heart I seek you;
 let me not wander from your *commandments*!
[11]In my heart I have stored up your *promise*,
 that I might not sin against you.
[12]Blessed are you, O Lord;
 teach me your *statutes*!

[13]With my lips I declare
 all the *judgments* of your mouth.
[14]In the way of your *testimonies* I rejoice
 as much as in all riches.
[15]On your *precepts* I will meditate
 and fix my eyes on your ways.
[16]In your *statutes* I will delight;
 I will not forget your word.

Like section 1, section 2 (Beth) seems to divide into four and four. Verses 9-12 focus on the word in the heart (vv. 10, 11); and then verses 13-16 follow that with the response of the lips.

A. THE WORD IN THE HEART: THE WORD IN THE HEART HAS
POWER TO KEEP US WALKING IN THE WAY OF THE WORD (VV. 9-12).

Verses 9-12 teach that the word that calls us to walk the way is
at the same time the word of his grace. This word can enter the
heart and enable us to walk this way. It comes from outside me
and weaves its way into my heart.

These verses sing the music of grace. There is a two-way
dynamic here. On the one hand he seeks the LORD with his 'whole
heart' (v. 10). He guards his path according to the word (v. 9).
On the other hand, he recognizes that he can only do this as that
promise is 'stored up' in his heart (v. 11). He knows that by nature
he will always 'wander from the commandments' (v. 10b). Only
the word in the heart can keep us in the way of the word.

A man told me once how he came to be a Christian. 'My
wife was a believer,' he said, 'and for her sake I used to go to
Bible studies. But I did not believe. And so my questions were
designed to catch the leader out, to trick the Christians, and to
show how clever I was and how stupid they were. But then a
year or so later I realized that my questions had changed. Now,
instead of tricking, instead of trying to prove myself right,
I realized I was asking because I wanted to know and desired to
follow. I realized that God's word had entered my heart.'

As he listened, read, and spoke the word of God, it entered
his heart. It did not enter his heart by some mystical short-cut.
It does not come sitting cross-legged with an empty mind in
front of a candle. It entered his heart by the only way words ever
enter the human heart, which is through the eye and the ear. It
is a wonderful thing that words in human language are God's
instrument to change the heart. But it is true, and we cannot
do without them. The evangelist Roger Carswell was teaching
at Cornhill, as he does most years. And he commented on
that unhelpful quotation of Francis of Assisi, who apparently
said, 'Preach the gospel; and if necessary, use words.' Roger
mischievously said that if he met Francis in heaven, he would
throttle him. And a Cornhill student piped up from the back

row (it had to be the back row), 'And if necessary, use hands!' That is right: words are necessary. They are God's chosen instrument, the sword of the Spirit to change the human heart.

It is a wonderful thing when that word does enter the heart. This is the amazement in the exclamation of verse 12: 'Blessed are you, O LORD; teach me your statutes!' That is, he prays, 'teach me to do them.' This is not like, 'Teach me the answers to the crossword or a Sudoku puzzle, that I may be clever and do well in a Bible study.' This is more like, 'Teach me to walk, that I may not wander or stumble.'

This psalm is about formation more than it is about information. It is about the habits that change the heart. For the word that first enters the heart in real Christian conversion goes on entering day by day and week by week when that word is preached and heard and read. It weaves its way into the fabric of our spirits, when we 'receive with meekness' that word that has already been 'implanted' in our hearts (James 1:21).

B. THE WORD ON THE LIPS: THE WORD IN THE HEART BUBBLES OUT THROUGH DELIGHTED LIPS (VV. 13-16).

There is a delightful movement here from the mouth of God to the heart of the believer and then on to the lips. The Covenant God speaks the word. That word is stored away in the heart. And that heart overflows into lips that declare with joy that Covenant word. The word translated 'rejoice' in verse 14 is 'a festive, exultant word' (Kidner). The theme here is of delight (vv. 14, 16) and meditation. To 'meditate' has the sense of musing or mulling over, usually by speaking the words aloud to myself. So the 'lips' here in verse 13 do not seem primarily to be speaking to others (as in evangelism); rather they are the believer reading aloud to himself or herself.

As the believer does this, it is a source of great delight. Three times in the psalm delight is associated with meditation on the word (here, in vv. 23, 24, and in vv. 47, 48). Meditation is a matter of delight because (and only because) the word is the word of his grace. If that was true for this old Covenant believer, how much more ought it to be true for us in whom the Spirit of God dwells forever.

I was speaking one day to a Korean who is a missionary in Japan. He told me (privately, not trying to impress, but to share a blessing) that it is his practice to read twenty chapters of scripture aloud to himself each day. He reads it aloud so that it is a multi-sensory experience. The word reaches him through his eyes as he reads, through his mouth as he forms the words, and through his ears as he hears. Every two months he gets through the whole Bible. And he said, 'It is such a blessing. I find that sometimes the words catch me', that is they catch hold of him, they take him by surprise, they ambush him with grace and joy, and they weave their way into his heart.

It would be good to learn from this Korean brother, as from our singer, to read the word of God aloud, so that we both hear and speak it. It is the word of Christ and therefore the word of grace. It is the word which alone has the power to change the human heart. So let us learn to sing this psalm. Let us believe that blessing comes by walking the way of the word. Let us long that we will walk that way with a whole heart. And let us not despair, but look to the word of his grace as we bow before it to receive it with meekness.

PERSONAL RESPONSE QUESTIONS

1. What habits and disciplines do you have in your life to guard your way according to his word and to store up his word of grace in your heart? Use this time to refresh and renew these disciplines.

2. How can you encourage the leadership of your church to make it a fellowship shaped and guarded by the word of God? What are the implications of this for the way we structure our Christian meetings, to give pride of place to the word God speaks into our hearts?

3

Section 3:
Pressure and Promise
(vv. 17-24)

Gimel

¹⁷Deal bountifully with your servant,
    that I may live and keep your *word*.
¹⁸Uncover my eyes, that I may behold
    wonders out of your *instruction*.
¹⁹A sojourner I am on the earth;
    hide not your *commandments* from me!
²⁰It wastes away, my soul, with longing
    for your *judgments* at all times.

²¹You rebuke the insolent, accursed ones,
    who wander from your *commandments*.
²²Take away from me scorn and contempt,
    for I have kept your *testimonies*.
²³Even though princes sit plotting against me,
    your servant will meditate on your *statutes*.
²⁴Your *testimonies* are my delight;
    they are my counsellors.

Sections 3 and 4 introduce the theme of hostility. They are tied together by two references to the LORD's 'wonders' (vv. 18, 27). This believer is no isolated academic living peacefully in some ivory tower. He is surrounded by enemies. In this way he foreshadows the Lord Jesus Christ and is a model for the believer of every age.

In Section 3 a new group of actors come onto the stage. So far it has just been the singer and his LORD. But now begins a theme that runs and runs in the psalm. The camera draws back from the place of prayer and reveals that it is set in the midst of a hostile world. Daniel prays; and his enemies watch to trap him (Dan. 6:10f). Jesus prays; and enemies wait to trap him (Mark 1:35; 3:6). This is the context of the believer and the word of God. If any group of Christian believers were to tell their stories, they would be stories of prayer in the midst of pressure. The music that now begins to play is the sound of threat and of rescue. And as we hear it we begin to understand why the word stored up in the heart is the safeguard against sin and wandering.

We are now reminded that the singer is 'on the earth' where he is 'a sojourner' (v. 19). And on this earth where he does not belong there are 'insolent, accursed' people (v. 21), who show him 'scorn and contempt' (v. 22) and some of whom are powerful ('princes' v. 23).

The section is bracketed by the words 'your servant' (vv. 17, 23). To say to the LORD, 'I am your servant' is not like the old-fashioned way of signing off a letter to *The Times*, 'your humble and obedient servant ...', which really didn't mean anything, and certainly not what it said. The title 'servant of the LORD' is a title of dignity. It means one who belongs to the LORD, who is bound to the LORD by bonds of Covenant, who is safely in the LORD's household, to whom the LORD is committed, and for whom the LORD has promised to act in rescue. He uses this title thirteen times in the psalm (vv. 17, 23, 38, 49, 65, 76, 84, 122, 124, 125, 135, 140, 176); in nine of these it is in the context of persecution and pressure.

Moses and the prophets are called the servants of the LORD. And in those wonderful prophetic passages in Isaiah 40-55, God calls the Lord Jesus Christ 'my servant'. This is a Covenant title that indicates a relationship of trust and dignity. The more forcefully and painfully danger asserts itself, the more precious becomes the singer's Covenant union with the LORD. All this is happening, he says, not just to 'poor little me' who just happens not to like it. No, it is happening to 'your servant', to whom you are deeply committed by Covenant.

The first half (vv. 17-20) is a desperate prayer. The second (vv. 21-24) tells us why it is so desperate. There is a logic linking the two.

A. WE MUST PRAY URGENTLY FOR GOD TO OPEN OUR EYES TO UNDERSTAND HIS WRITTEN WORD (VV. 17-20).

'Deal bountifully with (be generous to) your servant, that I may live and keep your word,' that is, that I may see blessing (as in vv. 1, 2). We will see in a moment why he might not live, why he might be crushed and destroyed. But let us notice first the reason he prays to live, which is 'that I may ... keep your word.' The grand purpose of his existence on this earth is to be a human being whose life is offered up in worship as he keeps the word and walks in the way. Why does he pray for life? Not so that he may enjoy self-centred pleasure, but that he may continue to worship with all his strength.

But how is God going to 'deal bountifully' with him? What action of God shows his grace and mercy? The answer is that he 'opens his eyes' (literally, rolls back the veil) to his word. In order to worship he needs his eyes opened. Verse 18 is a 'nugget' of gold: 'Uncover my eyes, that I may behold wonders out of your instruction.' Overwhelmingly in the Psalms, the 'wonders' of the LORD are his acts of Covenant rescue, provision and protection (e.g. Ps. 78:32). They are his rescue acts. Supremely they are the Exodus, the crossing of the Red Sea, and his provision for his people in the wilderness. These are the wonders that come out of his word, both because they are spoken in the first instance by his commanding word and because they are recorded and interpreted in his written word.

This prayer is not just that he will read any old amazing things in the Bible. He prays that his eyes will be opened to see and grasp that the God who rescued in the past is able to rescue him now. He wants deeply to understand that the Covenant LORD who acted in grace and steadfast love then is the same Covenant LORD today. Like Elisha's servant in 2 Kings 6:7, he needs the veil to be rolled back from his eyes to see the power of the unseen God to rescue him. And he sees this from the word.

This means of course that the 'word' in which he rejoices is not just the word we narrowly call 'Law', in the sense of the Ten Commandments and the other commandments that develop and apply them in the Old Testament. The 'word' here is the whole revelation of Law and Promise, of Law and Gospel, and therefore of Law and Christ. For Christ supremely is the wonderful deed of rescue. And so the veil over his eyes, as over ours, is only rolled back when we hope and trust in Christ (cf. 2 Cor. 3:12-18).

But why does he need to pray so passionately for this revealing, this unveiling of his eyes? The answer is in verse 19: 'A sojourner I am on the earth; hide not your commandments from me!' He is a sojourner, that is to say a resident alien, one who lives here but does not belong here. He has no territorial claim here in this age. He is passing through. He seeks that which is to come. He finds here no lasting city, but looks for a better one in the new age, the new creation (Heb. 11:10, 13-16).

Incidentally, even when the people of Israel possessed the Promised Land in the Middle East they still described themselves as sojourners in it. At the high point of their possession of it, Solomon could say, 'we are strangers before you and sojourners, as all our fathers were...' (1 Chron. 29:15). This was a way of recognizing that the promised land in the middle east was only a sign of the final resting place of the people of God. Even then they looked ahead for the city with foundations in the age to come.

Our problem is that the city of this age, the transient city, is very visible and tangible, experiential and intrusive with all its claims and idolatry. And therefore both he and we need our eyes opened to the word of God. For it is only in that word that we can see the unseen world to come, the city with foundations, the kingdom that cannot be shaken (Heb. 12:28).

I live in a house; but that house is not my home. I have a human family; but that family is not finally where I belong. I own possessions; yet those possessions are but what one person has called 'the travelling luggage of time'. I live in a world under judgment. Only the written word of God tells me that there are many rooms in the Father's house (John 14:2), that there is a city prepared for me, a city with foundations, in which God will dwell with his people. Only the written word of God tells me that I may be sure of that, that I may be a child of God, that I may be justified by faith, and that I may walk in the way everlasting.

I need my eyes opened to the word as 'wonder' if I am to keep the word as 'walk'. I need rescue and grace if I am to walk in the way. And I long for this: verse 20, 'It wastes away, my soul, with longing for your judgments at all times.' He is overwhelmed with an intense pining longing for the decisions of God in his favour as a believer. This is the strong feeling behind the prayers of verses 18 and 19: 'Uncover my eyes ... hide not your commandments..., because I long for this with all my heart. I am eaten up inside with this deep and desperate pining. No separated lover so pined for her beloved as I pine for what your word reveals to me.' This is an intense bodily hunger of heart.

But why can't we just pick up a Bible and read it? After all, we have brains. But it is important for us to realize that unless he rolls back the veil from my eyes, I will not and cannot see it. The reason we do not understand the Bible is not primarily that we lack the necessary intelligence. If that were so, then Christian maturity would be the preserve of the A* academics. But the reason is that we are sinners, and we need God to open our eyes.

As one writer has put it, 'the word of God is given but never possessed. Because it is God's instruction, it is not owned apart from the teaching of God. It is there, objectively available... But it must be sought and constantly studied in prayer in order to be taught...' This is right. I cannot understand the Bible apart from the Spirit of God who inspired it, because the purpose of the Bible is to draw and keep me in fellowship with God.

That is to say, the meaning of the word of God resides with God its author. He does not, as it were, plant the meaning in the text so that any human being may extract it. Nor certainly does he let the meaning reside with self-obsessed readers, for our eyes are so warped and twisted that the meaning we get will be 'spun' so that it affirms us in our present walk. No, the meaning of the word of God is only properly read from the word of God when the Author unlocks it by his Spirit to the reader who loves him and comes to him in humble dependence. The manner in which we approach the Bible is very important.

In his introduction to the Great Bible (the first officially sanctioned Bible in English), Cranmer wanted both to encourage its reading and warn of its abuse: 'Wherefore I would advise you all, that cometh to the reading or hearing of this book, which is the word of God, the most precious jewel, and most holy relic that remaineth upon earth, that ye bring with you the fear of God, and that ye do it with all due reverence, and use your knowledge thereof, not to vainglory or frivolous disputation, but to the honour of God, increase of virtue, and edification both of yourselves and others.'

It is not an empty formality that we begin our Bible studies with prayer. Unless God by his Spirit opens our eyes we cannot understand. We need to come to scripture on our knees, praying, 'Lord, teach me, teach me, teach me.' Not long after his conversion at Pembroke College, Oxford, the great eighteenth-century evangelist George Whitefield wrote in his journal, 'I began to read the Holy Scriptures upon my knees, laying aside all other books, and praying over, if possible, every line and word. This proved meat and drink indeed to my soul. I daily received fresh life, light and power from above.'

We must never approach Bible study with the arrogant omniscience of the ignorant, thinking, 'I know this passage; I have done this one before'. For God hides himself from clever-clever people, as he did supremely in the earthly ministry of Jesus, and he reveals himself to those of low status, 'children' in Bible imagery (Matt. 11:25).

And so this quality of the Bible draws us wonderfully into relationship. I read it. I want to grasp it, to gain insight, to understand. But I cannot do that simply by sitting there with it in front of me, studying it. It is his book, and the key to unlock it is in his hands. And therefore my desire to understand it leads me to the Keeper of the key. The very nature of the Bible draws me into loving dependence upon him.

We need to pray for this uncovering to happen. Specifically we need to pray that when we read of his rescues in history, the spark will jump from scripture to our hearts and we will grasp that he has the power to rescue me now. For example, I read of the Lord Jesus raising the dead and I grasp that he has the authority to raise my body on the last day. This understanding is a supernatural thing. Most Christians have at some stage of their lives heard the story of the Cross, for example, and been untouched by it. We need to pray that when we hear the story of redemption, we will grasp that this does not just mean he has done something in the past, but that because of this he can rescue us in the present. It is for this he prays.

But why does the singer feel so deeply that he needs this understanding? The answer – and it comes as a surprise – is found in the second half of this section.

B. WE URGENTLY NEED THIS UNDERSTANDING BECAUSE THE WORD OF GOD IS OUR ONLY RELIABLE COUNSEL IN A HOSTILE WORLD (VV. 21-24).

We have had a hint of what we are coming to, in verse 19a: 'I am a sojourner on the earth'. I don't belong here. And to get me through my sojourn, my stay on earth, I need to know God's word. But why is being a sojourner such a dangerous state? Verses 21-24 tell us.

Bible Delight

The 'insolent' of verse 21 appear many more times in the psalm (vv. 51, 69, 78, 85, 122). They are presumptuous, proud, and self-sufficient. They are going through this world on their own, thank you very much. I was speaking with a Buddhist and we were discussing the need for love in the world. I said to him, perhaps tactlessly, that I was sorry he had no God to love him. He replied somewhat defensively that in Buddhism, 'we generate the love from within ourselves'. But any attitude that thinks we can conjure up from within ourselves the moral resources that we and the world need, is categorised by the Bible as a form of arrogance.

We meet these people here in three aspects. Towards the godly they are insolent. Under God they are accursed. And in themselves they wander from the commandments. They are not walking in the way; but they harass those who are. They are proud, presumptuous, rebellious, full of themselves, empty of God and hostile to the godly. They deride the singer (v. 51), smear him with lies (vv. 69, 78), dig pits to make him fall (v. 85) and oppress him (v. 122). And they 'wander' (cf. v. 118), exactly as the singer has prayed not to do (v. 1).

Every man or woman who seeks God and walks by his written word will inevitably be despised, scorned and troubled by men and women who do not. So the moment I direct my life, orientate my life, set the arrow of my life wholeheartedly to go the way of God's word, I make myself enemies. I cannot help it. 'The world will hate you', says Jesus (John 15:18, 19).

Our brother feels the pain of their scorn (v. 22): 'Take away from me scorn and contempt, for I have kept your testimonies'. This is not a self-righteous claim, but a true claim to be a believer, a man who is faithful to the Covenant. 'Because I belong to you they scorn me,' he says, 'They look down on me, they count me a nobody.' He knows what it is to see the raised eyebrow of surprise: you believe that, do you? How odd! Or the curled lip of the sneer: Bible basher, ignorant fundamentalist. Or the cold shoulder of being cut out from the party round, excluded from the in-group, or passed over for the deserved promotion.

Pressure and Promise (vv. 17-24)

How he longs for that injustice to be reversed. And the only place where he finds reassurance that one day it will be is in God's word. Verse 23: 'Even though princes sit plotting against me, your servant will meditate on your statutes. Your testimonies are my delight; they are my counsellors.' The word 'princes' is a general purpose Old Testament word for powerful people, rather as we used to speak of 'The Barons of Fleet Street' or 'Captains of Industry'. The believer is so weak; all he has, in our terms, is the word of the Cross (1 Cor. 1:18). But these are men of weight and influence. They sit plotting against him. And yet he does not meditate on them. He does not let his waking moments be dominated by their threats. No, he meditates on the Covenant statutes of God. These statutes give him wisdom. They open his eyes to what lasts and what is really worth fearing. And they expose to him the fragile nature of this age with all its power and pretension. It is for this reason that meditation on the statutes (v. 23) is associated here with delight (v. 24) (as also in vv. 15, 16 and vv. 47, 48). Meditation on scripture is not a sombre business even though it takes place in a dark world.

Because of the pressure of a hostile world he understands that he must have his eyes opened to the word of God. For these words 'are my counsellors'. And unless you open my eyes to grasp the meaning of your word, I won't survive.

And so in this third section we see how the word ties us to reality, to the age to come, because out of the word we see the wonders of God's rescue in the past. And out of the word we are assured that these are anticipations of his wonderful deed of rescue in the future, the redemption of our bodies. That's why (v. 20) I find in my body this aching longing for your judgments, for the reality to which your word points. For I find in your word that you have acted in judgment, you have ruled against the arrogant and in favour of the faithful. And I hold on to that even as I cry out, 'How long, O Lord?'

One day that judgment will be final, irreversible and solid in present experience. But before that, there is a long journey with our singer through much pain and issuing in yet deeper prayer. In this journey the word of God will prove to be his lifeline, his counselors to guide him (v. 24). And because he has thrown in his lot wholeheartedly this way, he desperately needs to understand this word.

So the motivation for the singer's heartfelt cry to have his eyes opened is the pressure of hostility from the world around. The process is this: I am drawn by the grace of God to seek him and walk in the ways of his word. The world begins to oppose me, to scorn me, to plot against me. And so as I read his word I pray with all my heart for God to open my eyes to understand it. For these words are my only reliable counsellors. And so the process of hostility is turned by God into a pressure that squeezes me closer to the God I seek.

PERSONAL RESPONSE QUESTIONS

1. Do you pray from the heart for God to open your eyes when you read or hear his word? What from this section will motivate you to mean this prayer?

2. How can you prevent yourself from becoming obsessed with your problems, and instead train yourself to meditate on his word?

4

Section 4:
The Word of Freedom
(vv. 25-32)

Daleth

[25]My soul clings to the dust;
  give me life according to your *word*!
[26]When I told of my ways, you answered me;
  teach me your *statutes*!
[27]Make me understand the way of your *precepts*,
  and I will meditate on your wonders.
[28]My soul melts away for sorrow;
  strengthen me according to your *word*!

[29]Put false ways far from me
  and graciously (teach me) your *instruction*!
[30]I have chosen the way of faithfulness;
  I set your *judgments* before me.
[31]I cling to your *testimonies*, O LORD;
  let me not be put to shame!
[32]I will run in the way of your *commandments*
  when you enlarge my heart!

This section begins in the dust and ends in a wide place. This is significant for Christian experience.

It divides naturally into two parts. Verses 25-28 are bracketed with suffering; verses 29-32 with grace. The division is even

clearer in the Hebrew, where verses 25-28 all end with one Hebrew letter (*kaph*), and verses 29-32 all end with another (*yodh*).
In each half there is a clinging (vv. 25, 31). We will look at the
two parts separately and then hold them together.

A. THE WORD OF GOD IS OUR ONLY HOPE IN SUFFERING
(VV. 25-28).

Notice how similar are verse 25 and verse 28. Verse 25a, 'My
soul clings to the dust' is closely parallel to verse 28a, 'My soul
melts away for sorrow.' And again, verse 25b, 'give me life
according to your word' is very similar to verse 28b, 'strengthen
me according to your word.'

In the first half of this section we feel more passionately than
ever the pain of the singer. His soul (i.e. he himself) clings to
the dust. That is, the soul that came from the dust of the earth
feels it is about to return to that dust according to the curse of
Genesis 3:19. 'I am flat on my face in the dust, laid low, stuck
in the mud, mired; I cannot break free from the dust of death
except by the word.' (NIV 'laid low' misses the stickiness and
inability to get up, and the word echo of 'cling' in v. 31.) And
so he prays, 'give me life according to your word.' This word
is the word of promise, the word of the gospel, and the word
of Christ. It promises an unbreakable connection between the
believer and the God who is not the God of the dead but of the
living (Matt. 22:32). And therefore it is the word of resurrection.

It is because of this unbreakable connection of Covenant
that he can say in verse 26, 'When I told of my ways you
answered me', that is, 'when I appealed as your covenant
servant, according to your word of promise, I told of my ways,
my heart desire to walk with you in the way, then you answered
me – as you always will, as you have promised to do.' This is not
self-righteousness ('Lord, look how good I am'). Rather, this is
an honest opening of the life before God. It may also have the
sense of telling of his wayward ways in repentance, and asking

for restoration (cf. v. 59). As God looks at my life he will see that, weak and poor as I am, I do belong to him, I am his child, I am a believer.

And so, again (v. 26b) 'teach me your statutes', teach me to walk in your ways. At every stage there is a conscious urgent dependency on grace. Verse 27: 'Make me understand' (grasp, really get hold of) 'the way of your precepts, and I will meditate on your wonders'. Notice again how the way of his precepts, the godly walk, is inseparable from his wonders, the wonders of his grace and rescue (as in v. 18).

And then verse 28 echoes verse 25: 'My soul melts away for sorrow; strengthen me according to your word.' That is, my inner person is like a house that leaks' (cf. the same 'melts' word in Eccles. 10:18), or eyes that pour out tears' (the same 'melt' word is used in Job 16:20). As the King James Version put it, 'My soul melteth for heaviness.' He says, 'I have collapsed with intense sorrow. I am desperate.' And so in verses 25-28 he is nearly dead and he feels himself deeply a mortal under the curse of Genesis 3.

But the word of God reveals to him the wonder of the gospel, that God answers the cry of the dying sinner who calls out in penitence. He prays in verse 25b and verse 28b for life and strength 'according to your word'. He doesn't just cry out, 'Lord, this is grim; please help.' No, he claims the word and promise of God, in which God commits himself to everyone who calls on his name.

But for what does he call? The answer in verses 29-32 may be surprising. We instinctively pray that our circumstances will change and the pressures be relieved. We pray that both for ourselves and for others. Instead he prays for solidity of character, for straightness. He realizes that the deepest danger he faces is not that he will be crushed by his enemies but that he will be jellified and go soft. His greatest threat is not the power of his enemies but their seduction. Perhaps he remembers that the people of Israel were unharmed by Balaam's curses, which God turned into blessing (Num. 22–24); but they were destroyed by his seduction (Num. 25 with Num. 31:16). They were safe in the face of a curse, but they went soft when lured by seduction. The word of God promises us rescue in the end. But in the present it promises us steadfastness in the midst of suffering.

B. The grace of God brings us into a wide place of freedom in the midst of suffering (vv. 29-32).

This second half is bracketed by grace: verse 29b, 'graciously (teach me) your instruction!'; verse 32b, '...when you enlarge my heart' (literally, 'open wide my heart'). Grace does not remove pressure from us. Grace keeps us going straight under pressure. This is why in verse 29 he prays, 'Put false ways from me' – the way of the lie, the way of faithlessness – 'and graciously teach me your instruction', literally, 'bless me, be gracious to me with your instruction'. The law is the antidote to the lie. The law in the heart brings truth in the inward parts. It counteracts spin with integrity, and pretence with honesty.

Because he is so concerned to avoid 'false ways', he prays in verse 30, 'I have chosen the way of faithfulness', that is, honesty and steadiness, not moral jelly. 'I set your judgments before me.' Human life is always, as has been said, 'where two ways meet'. At every point of life we make choices. And if we are to choose and go on choosing, the way of faithfulness, we need to set before us the moral decisions God makes, that we may make them too.

And so in verse 31, the soul that *clings* to the dust of death in verse 25 now *clings* also to the testimonies of God. 'Let me not be put to shame.' As in verse 6, what he most dreads is that in the last day he will be put to shame. He will be publicly seen as a fraud. He fears that all his claims to be a child of God will be seen to be false and he himself exposed to shame and scorn.

And so he clings to the Covenant testimonies of God to hold him fast. Perhaps in a shadowy way he even knows by the

The Word of Freedom (vv. 25-32)

Spirit of God that his hope will not disappoint him because of the Covenant love of God poured into his heart by the Spirit (cf. Rom. 5:5).

The section that began with the singer flat on his face in sticky mud (v. 25), ends with him running free (v. 32). 'I will run in the way of your commandments when you enlarge my heart.' There is something very similar in verse 45, 'I will walk in a wide place', a large, free place. The word 'wide' in verse 45 is from the same word group as that translated 'enlarge' in verse 32.

It is one of the paradoxes of the world, that sin promises freedom but enslaves. And the law of God seems to promise constraint but opens the heart to a free wild joyful run, while at the same time he is flat on his face in the dust. This is Christian experience. The word opens my mind to wisdom, to a wide interest in the whole world, as it did with Solomon's 'breadth of mind'. It opens my emotions to a free joyful running. The famous quotation of the Olympic runner Eric Liddell takes on a new meaning here: 'When I run, I feel (God's) pleasure.'

H. G. Wells, the visionary science-fiction writer, was a bitter opponent of Christianity. But in 1937, at a party given for his seventy-first birthday, he announced to his guests, 'Gentlemen, I am 71 years old today and I have never found peace. The trouble with people like me is that the man from Galilee, Jesus of Nazareth, was too big for my small heart.' It was a candid admission.

The word of God opens up to us under pressure a joyful free running, the ability to forgive and go on forgiving, the ability to live without being eaten up by resentment, the ability to bear up under pressure, under those hard submissions to which all Christians are called. The law of God and the Lord Jesus Christ enlarge the heart and open the life of the disciple to run free in the midst of pressure. This is the experience of the singer. He runs free while at the same time he is at death's door. He is kept solid and steady in the inner man while melting and wasting away in the body (2 Cor. 4:16). He clings to the dust of death; and yet he runs in the way of life. It is one of the great paradoxes of the Christian life that it brings this freedom in the midst of tough times.

This freedom comes from walking with a clear conscience. It comes from spiritual solidity in the midst of moral jelly. It comes not from circumstances that have been made easier, but from an inner life that has been made stronger. So that by the word of God in the heart he is made firm under pressure.

PERSONAL RESPONSE QUESTIONS

1. Have there been times in your life when you have been conscious both of 'clinging to the dust' and also of 'clinging to his testimonies' (in the language of this section)? How can you hold these together?

2. What experience do you have of the word of God enlarging your heart so that you can run free in the midst of the pressures of life?

5

Section 5:
The Word of Life
(vv. 33-40)

He

33Teach me, O LORD, the way of your *statutes*;
and I will keep it to the end.
34Give me understanding, that I may keep your *instruction*
and observe it with my whole heart.
35Lead me in the path of your *commandments*,
for I delight in it.
36Incline my heart to your *testimonies*,
and not to selfish gain!

37Turn my eyes from looking at worthless things;
and in your ways give me life.
38Confirm to your servant your *promise*,
that you may be feared.
39Turn away the reproach that I dread,
for your *judgments* are good.
40Behold, I long for your *precepts*;
in your righteousness give me life!

I am not sure that this section has a clear structure. But I think we may again divide it into two equal parts, with the second half bracketed by the petition 'give me life' (vv. 37b, 40b). The first half is a sustained prayer in two pairs: 'teach me ... give me understanding ... lead me ... incline my heart...'

A. WE MAY PRAY WITH CONFIDENCE FOR BIBLE UNDER-
STANDING ONLY WHEN OUR HEART IS DETERMINED TOWARDS
BIBLE OBEDIENCE (VV. 33-36).

Verse 33 and verse 34 say much the same thing in parallel for emphasis. They both begin with a plea for Bible understanding (v. 33a, 'Teach me, O LORD, the way of your statutes ...'; verse 34a, 'Give me understanding ...') and they both go on to a promise of Bible obedience (v. 33b, '... and I will keep it to the end' and then verse 34, '... that I may keep your instruction and observe it with my whole heart').

If there is a movement, it is that the second verse (v. 34) increases the emphasis on the Bible obedience, replacing the simple '... keep it to the end' with the expanded, '... that I may keep your instruction and observe it with my whole heart.' So the movement of the two is to say, 'I want to understand the Bible so that I can keep it. What I mean is that I want to understand it so that I *really will* keep it with my whole heart.' We begin with the plea for understanding and end on the note of wholehearted obedience.

The logic is this. If I ask God to show me what the Bible means just because I am interested, or because I want to have better Bible knowledge and get a bit more credibility in my church, or become an academic biblical scholar, then I can have no confidence that God will answer my prayer. For the purpose of his statutes (v. 33a) is to lead me into the *way* of his statutes, which is a changed direction and shape of life. It is like asking a local resident the way to the station; and he gives me written instructions; and in front of him I tear up his instructions. And then I ask him again. He is not going to waste his time telling me again, any more than God is going to open my eyes to understand a word I have no intention of obeying.

The Word of Life (vv. 33-40)

And therefore only when my heart is fixed on going his way can I pray the prayer for understanding with confidence that God will answer. Or, to put it another way, I will only grow in Bible knowledge when I walk in Bible obedience. This is why in verse 35 he prays not just for understanding but to be led 'in the *path* of your commandments' because he delights in them, that is he really wants to walk that path.

The fact that Bible understanding is more a moral than an intellectual matter is reinforced by the – to us – surprising pair of opposites in verse 36: 'Incline (or turn) my heart to your testimonies, and not to selfish gain' (or unfair, unjust gain). This is both challenging and encouraging. It is a challenge to repentance and faith. But it is also encouraging.

This means that the opposite of a heart that will understand the Bible is not a heart that is unintelligent or a heart that doesn't know Greek and Hebrew (valuable as these are) or a heart that is tired and can't concentrate very well.

No, the opposite of a heart that will understand the Bible is a heart that is turned towards feathering its own nest, making its own way in the world, even if it means trampling on others in the process. The only block that will stop us understanding the Bible is a desire for selfish gain. If that is my heart, that is what makes me tick (never mind if I have some kind of Christian veneer over it), then I will never understand the Bible. To understand the Bible I need a heart that is turned towards *doing* God's testimonies with my feet, my lips, my wallet, and my hands. It is not enough just to have a mind that wants to *know* God's testimonies in my head.

The second half of this section motivates me to have this heart desire to go God's way.

B. A HEART DIRECTED TOWARDS BIBLE OBEDIENCE IS A HEART DIRECTED TOWARDS LIFE RATHER THAN EMPTINESS (VV. 37-40).

The second half is held together by the plea, 'give me life' in verse 37 and verse 40, and by the repeated 'turn ... from/away' in verses 37 and 39. A double turning away from evil leads to a double turning towards life. There is a subtle change of contrast in verses 37-40. In verses 33-36 the connection is between Bible understanding and Bible obedience. Now the focus is on life as opposed to emptiness.

Notice how the section is bracketed:

> Verse 37 'Turn my eyes (that is, my desires, my orientation, what makes me tick) from looking at worthless things; and *give me life* in your ways'
>
> Verse 40b '... in your righteousness *give me life*'

Those two phrases 'give me life' translate the same word in verse 37 and verse 40, and in each case they are the last word of the verse. So this section is about life by God's word and grace.

The section begins with a prayer not to direct his life, his desires, towards 'worthless things'. The word means 'vanity' or 'emptiness'. This is the great Old Testament idea that an idol, any project or person to whom or which I am devoted, to which I give my energy and time and affections, any such project or person that is not the living God, is an idol. He has understood that the two paths open to every human being are one that is substantial and one that is empty.

Archbishop William Temple once compared British society to a shop window in which the price tags had been changed around. Things of no worth are priced dear; and things of great worth are counted as dirt. Falsehood, the clever crook, Enron, the successful corrupt, the sexual winner, the financial wheeler-dealer, the celebrity, all are priced high. We paint as valuable that which is empty. But when did we last read a magazine article extolling the value of self-control? The fruit of the Spirit is counted as dirt. But the word of God makes me love goodness and appreciate its value. It is a good illustration. An idol sells itself dear. Whether it be career success or sexual fulfilment or popularity or self-esteem, it says it is valuable and worth a big investment of my energies. Indeed it demands a big investment; idols do not come cheap. But actually an idol is empty.

An idol promises much in this age but delivers nothing of lasting value in the age to come. It is an emptiness, a nothing, a weightlessness, a vapour, a will o' the wisp, something that just blows away in the wind of judgment like chaff. Those who worship idols become like them (Ps. 115:8). If I bow down to emptiness, then I myself will become empty. The worship of idols is the most successful form of weight loss in the world. I worship until I just fade away. I may be physically obese while being spiritually weightless. The singer prays that his eyes will be turned from looking at, and desiring, empty things.

By contrast he prays (v. 37b) for *life*, real, substantial, ever-lasting, joy-filled life in God's ways. God's 'ways' here means his word, his instruction. This is one of the four verses with a substitute for the regular 'word' words. And so he prays for perseverance (v. 38), he prays to be 'confirmed' or 'made firm' by the promise of God, into a life lived in reverent fear of God (v. 38b). Ultimately, a life that looks at and desires empty things will be a life that ends in shame or reproach (v. 39).

One of the paradoxes with which many Christian workers struggle is that we devote our energies to something which in the eyes of others is a worthless and empty thing, because it is just words on a page. People think how stupid we are to take risks and devote our lives to something like that. Why not do something more substantial, get a better house, a proper job, a career?

Martin Luther wrote on verse 36, 'Why else is it that the Holy Scriptures have already for a long time been despised, especially in our age, while the legal profession, the arts, and philosophy [we might want to add some other] have been intensively cultivated, if not because the latter have to do with acquiring bread, [and we might want to add butter and jam] while the former are for the poor? If the arts and the legal profession would yield as little earthly gain as Holy Scripture gives, they would quickly vanish and be neglected. Again, if Scripture were profitable (that is, in money terms), nothing would be more cultivated and resorted to.'

The singer has understood that to follow scripture is actually to follow substance. In a world that thinks exactly the opposite, he prays that he will delight in the word rather than the world. He knows that if he loves the world then love for the Father is not in him (1 John 2:15-17). This is the prayer of a weak but realistic believer. Teach me, lead me, turn me, make me firm. Because the moment you leave me to my own desires I will turn aside after worthless things.

As we sing this section, we need to pray for a work of the Spirit of God in our hearts to change our desires, to redirect our affections, so that he turn our eyes from gazing longingly at worthless things. Then he will make us firm in his promise and give us substantial life.

Personal Response Questions

1. To what 'worthless things' or 'selfish gain' are you particularly vulnerable in your desires?

2. How will this section move you to a heart turned instead to the word and values of God?

6

Section 6:
The Wide Word
(vv. 41-48)

Waw

⁴¹Let your steadfast love come to me, O Lᴏʀᴅ,
   your salvation according to your *promise*;
⁴²then shall I have an answer for him who taunts me,
   for I trust in your *word*.

⁴³And take not the word of truth utterly out of my mouth,
   for my hope is in your *judgments*.
⁴⁴I will keep your *instruction* continually,
   forever and in perpetuity,

⁴⁵and I shall walk in a wide place,
   for I have sought your *precepts*.
⁴⁶I will also speak of your *testimonies* before kings
   and shall not be put to shame,

⁴⁷and I find my delight in your *commandments*,
   which I love.
⁴⁸I will lift up my hands toward your *commandments*,
   which I love,
      and I will meditate on your *statutes*.

There seems to be a movement in this sixth section. I think it
most naturally falls into four couplets, as follows.

A. We may pray confidently for Covenant rescue (vv. 41, 42).

'Steadfast love' translates an important Old Testament word, and it is the first time it is used in this psalm (cf. vv. 76, 88, 124, 149, 159). It doesn't just mean that God is a nice chap, a loving, decent, generous sort of God. It has a more precise meaning. It means what we sometimes call 'Covenant love', that is, love in the framework of a clearly stated agreement. God's Covenant of grace is his promise to all who belong to him that he will be our God and we will be his people. To all who come into and belong to that people, he pledges his Covenant love, his steadfast love.

So when the singer prays for the Lord's 'steadfast love' to come to him he is not asking a favour but claiming the promise of the Covenant. This is why in verse 41b he asks the same thing in a parallel way and calls it 'your salvation (that is, rescue) *according to your promise*'. The Covenant promises are found in the Covenant document, which is the written word of scripture. This is why scripture is so precious, because it is the precious and very great promises of God (2 Pet. 1:4). He prays for rescue in his suffering. And he does so using the great Covenant promise word of 'steadfast love'. We may do the same.

He puts 'steadfast love' in parallel with 'your salvation'. That is, he prays for more than a subjective feeling of comfort, but rather a concrete experience of rescue in some way, a 'salvation'. And when this salvation comes he will have 'an answer for the one who taunts' him.

What does this mean? Who taunts him and why? In our terms the one who taunts him is the hard-headed neighbour or work colleague, who says things like, 'This Christian business is all a bit stupid. You're a pretty fool to trust in a God you can't see. You need to be more careful. You trust in God; let's see if God will deliver you. Oh, it doesn't look as if he's going to; silly you! How foolish you are to believe.'

There will be times when the Christian will do things that make no sense to the unbeliever at all. They just think, 'That is going to be a complete waste.' We see that sometimes when a young Christian wants to go into Christian service. Maybe he or she has a good degree from a decent university; and the parents (especially the father) can't help feeling that he or she is wasting their life.

It has always been like this for the one who trusts the unseen God. No doubt Noah, the herald of righteousness (2 Pet. 2:5) was mocked mercilessly for the foolishness of building the Ark. He had only the promise to go on. And no doubt he longed to be able to give an answer to the one who taunted him. And then the judgment came, and there was his terrible answer.

The wavering believer of Psalm 73 must have felt like this as he listened to the arrogant scoffing of the ungodly (vv. 8, 9). 'They tell me there's no point following God; and I am beginning to think they were right.' He must have longed to have an answer for the one who mocked.

Likewise the righteous in the days of Malachi must have longed to be able to give an answer to those who said there was no point believing, since, 'Everyone who does evil is good in the sight of the LORD, and he delights in them' (Mal. 2:17). It doesn't seem that God cares, they said. There doesn't seem any point in being a believer. How they must have longed for the LORD suddenly to come to his Temple (Mal. 3:1).

Above all, how the Lord Jesus must have longed to be able to give an answer to those who mocked him on the Cross: 'He trusts in God; let God deliver him, if he desires him' (but he doesn't seem to) (Matt. 27:43). Jesus' answer came on the first Easter morning, when God declared before the universe that this was his beloved Son to whom all authority in heaven and on earth is entrusted. As the singer trusted in 'your word' (v. 42) so Jesus entrusted himself to him who judges justly (1 Pet. 2:23); and his trust was not in vain.

The singer longs for 'an answer', a proof that the risks he is taking are not empty, that the unseen God does exist and does reward those who seek him (Heb. 11:6) Likewise for the believer today, while heaven is silent there is no answer to the taunt. But when God rescues, then there will be an answer. Sometimes there is a partial answer in this life. Always it will come at the end, in the judgment.

This raises for us the link between what I call little rescues and the Big Rescue. Every time a prayer is answered we are given a little rescue. A stressed young mother prays for and finds a parking space. That is a little rescue: real, but little. A sick person prays for healing and is healed. That is a little rescue: not so little, and very real, but still little. When Lazarus was raised from the dead, it was a little rescue. Quite a big little rescue (!), but still an anticipatory rescue and not the final rescue, since Lazarus must later have died.

All these little rescues are signposts forward to the Big Rescue. 'I am the Resurrection and the Life; he who believes in me shall live, even though he die' (John 11:25). That is the Big Rescue for which the singer longs. That will be the final answer to him who taunts, when the people who thought they were really weighty and significant in the world will be blown away like chaff. And the people the world thought were insignificant feel that gentle hand on the head, and hear the words, 'This is my son, my daughter; this one belongs to me.' Then there will be an answer for the one who taunts.

So in his trial the singer prays for rescue. He prays for it on the basis of Covenant promise, praying for 'steadfast (Covenant) love' to 'the LORD', the Covenant God, 'according to your (Covenant) promise', 'for I trust in your word'. So even in the darkness he can look forward with confidence, a confidence based not on present evidence of rescue but simply on the pledged word of the faithful Covenant God.

B. WE MAY PRAY CONFIDENTLY TO BE KEPT PERSEVERING TO THE END UNTIL THE RESCUE COMES (VV. 43, 44).

As he looks forward to rescue, he prays something closely related. He knows God will rescue all who are his. But he needs also to pray that on that day he will still be his. And so he prays for his own perseverance. Verse 43, 'And take not the word of truth (that is, the Covenant word) utterly out of my mouth (which is much the same as verse 8, 'do not forsake me deeply'), for my hope is in your judgments.' This is another example where the word translated 'judgments' has a grace meaning; he hopes in those judgments, putting his trust that the legal decisions made by the judge of all the earth will be made in his favour.

What does he mean by praying for the word of truth not to be taken utterly out of his mouth? I think the meaning is that so long as it is in his mouth it is in his heart. So long as he continues to speak it, read it, proclaim it, and delight in it, so long he continues to walk the way of the Lord, and therefore so long he is headed for rescue. And as he trusts in this sustaining grace he can go on (v. 44) to say, 'I will keep your instruction continually, forever and in perpetuity.' That is, you will keep me firm that I may endure to the end and be saved (Mark 13:13).

C. WE MAY PRAY CONFIDENTLY FOR A BOLD TESTIMONY AND MINISTRY UNDER PRESSURE (VV. 45, 46).

The first couplet is a prayer for rescue. The second is a prayer for perseverance until that rescue. The third couplet expresses a confidence that as he perseveres he will experience a paradoxical freedom in his witness for God.

> Verse 45: 'And I shall walk in *a wide place* (the same word group as v. 32 'when you enlarge my heart') for I have sought your precepts.

> Verse 46: I will also speak of your testimonies *before kings* and shall not be put to shame.'

These two verses fit together. In his tough discipleship he is confident that hanging on to the word of promise does more than guarantee future vindication. Paradoxically it also leads to present freedom even in chains. 'I shall walk in a wide place;

even as my enemies hem me in on every side I walk in a wide place. Even as they chain me, I will have a wide audience of kings.' Even as princes sit plotting against him (v. 23), his ministry will widen and widen. This is a very practical truth: it is precisely when we are squeezed by pressure that our ministry grows. When there is no pressure, when our Christian service comes at no cost, it doesn't grow. But it is precisely when we are under pressure that it grows.

When the Lord Jesus himself stood in the tight corner of Pilate's dock, he was able to speak his testimony before kings. He was not put to shame. In fact, as he stood trial, it was Pilate and Jesus' enemies who were actually on trial. In Acts 4 we see the apostles under pressure, constrained by powerful opposition; and yet they speak the word of God with all boldness in a wide place of freedom. At his conversion Paul is told he must bear Jesus' name before kings (Acts 9:15). And this comes true only when he is a prisoner in Acts 24–26, and above all in Caesar's court (Acts 28; Phil. 1:12-14; 2 Tim. 4:17). And in that tight spot, as we say, his ministry is liberated and becomes a paradoxical 'wide place'. It has always been like this, and no doubt it will always be.

I read recently a historical novel about Perpetua and the little group of courageous early Christian martyrs, killed on Caesar's birthday in Carthage in the second century. The novelist perceptively portrayed a Centurion watching their deaths. And as they died, he realized that he with his freedom was in chains whereas they in their chains were free and victorious. As the martyrs died, he knew they had won the victory over Caesar.

There is no short-cut for this. It is when we are under pressure and adversity that we hold on to the promises and our work for Christ can grow.

D. WE SHOULD LOVE THE WORD OF GOD THAT GIVES US THIS CONFIDENCE (VV. 47, 48).

The fourth couplet culminates the progression with a wonderful expression of love and delight. Verses 47, 48 are tied by the repeated clause 'which I love'. (We have seen this combination of delight and meditation in vv. 15, 16 and in vv. 23, 24.) Verse 48 has two of the regular eight 'word' words for emphasis.

Strictly speaking, we would think that we ought not to speak of loving the Bible, but should rather reserve our love for the Lord. We are nervous about loving the word of the Lord instead of loving the Lord of the word. And yet the singer here unashamedly says he loves 'your commandments'. His desire and his affection are warmly directed towards this wonderful word that gives him freedom in prison, a wide ministry in opposition, and points surely to the day when the final answer will be given to all who taunt him.

We too will love the Bible. For it assures us of rescue in the end; it assures us of grace to persevere to the end; and it assures us of a bold, free testimony on the way to the end. And so in this section we see how a love for the word of God opens up a wide pathway to free bold witness in the midst of suffering. It can do this because it assures us of our security. And therefore it begins to be God's antidote to the fear of man. After all, if I know God is for me then I may confidently say, 'What can man do to me?' (Heb. 13:6).

In all this, we see that it is pressure that presses us back upon the promises of God. And as we cling to those promises, we may pray confidently for rescue, for perseverance until rescue comes, and for a wide and fruitful ministry for Christ. No wonder he rejoices in and loves this word.

PERSONAL RESPONSE QUESTIONS

1. What experience do you have of being thought silly for being a Christian (i.e. 'him who taunts')?

2. Do you have any experience of 'little rescues' (answers to prayer in this life) which begin to answer your mockers? What if those 'little rescues' don't come?

7

Section 7:
Comfort and Songs in the Night
(vv. 49-56)

Zayin

⁴⁹Remember your *word* to your servant,
   in which you have made me hope.
⁵⁰This is my comfort in my affliction,
   that your *promise* gives me life.

⁵¹The insolent utterly deride me,
   but I do not turn away from your *instruction*.
⁵²When I remember your *judgments* from of old,
   O Lord, I take comfort.

⁵³Hot indignation seizes me because of the wicked,
   who turn away from your *instruction*.
⁵⁴Your *statutes* have been my songs
   in the house of my sojourning.

⁵⁵I remember your name in the night, O Lord,
   and keep your *instruction*.
⁵⁶This blessing has fallen to me,
   that I have kept your *precepts*.

The tone for this section is set by the repeated words 'remember' (vv. 49, 52, 55), which begins with the Hebrew letter *zayin*, and 'comfort' (vv. 50, 52). As he himself remembers the judgments and name of the LORD, so he calls on the LORD to remember his Covenant word. This double remembering brings him comfort and songs in the night (vv. 54, 55). In verse 50 there is the first mention in this psalm of the important word 'affliction'. And in verses 51, 53 there is a repetition of 'turn away'.

The section falls into four couplets. Apart from the first, there is a degree of parallelism, each beginning with pressure ('the insolent' in v. 51, 'the wicked' in v. 53, and 'the night' in v. 55) and ending with hope ('comfort' in v. 52, 'songs' in v. 54, and 'blessing' in v. 56). A positive emphasis is set by the first couplet, with its mentions of 'hope', 'comfort' and 'life', and by the last verse with its focus on 'blessing'. In the context of being a 'sojourner' (v. 19), not belonging in a hostile world (vv. 21-23), he clings to the promise of the Covenant God and finds comfort and songs in the night.

A. WE TAKE COMFORT FROM THE COVENANT PROMISES (vv. 49, 50).

To ask the Covenant God to 'remember' (v. 49) does not suggest that he has amnesia. To 'remember' is more than cognitive recall. Although we typically speak of remembering a fact to put down in an exam, to 'remember' in scripture means to recall some truth with a view to taking action arising from it. Here we ask the LORD to act in accordance with his Covenant obligations. When the LORD remembers his word it is not that he wakes in the morning and thinks, 'Oh, yes, I'd forgotten, but now I remember that I love them and have made them a promise.' To remember his word means to act on the promise he has never forgotten, that is, to put the promise into effect. Again (as in v. 17) the singer calls himself 'your servant', another reminder of Covenant security. And so he calls on the LORD to do what he has promised to do, to 'remember his word'.

But although the delay is painful, he understands that it does not nullify the promise. Indeed, he has grasped that God deliberately makes us hope ('you have made me hope' v. 49), or wait (for the word means both, cf. vv. 74, 81, 114, 147), for the fulfilment of the promise. It is his plan that we learn obedience through suffering in hope (cf. Heb. 5:8). It is the plan of God that the believer hold on in hope; God calls us to this patient waiting.

So now he pleads with the LORD to act, to remember. In the midst of his 'affliction' (v. 50) this word of promise is his 'comfort', this word of promise that assures him that he has life and will one day experience eternal life in the resurrection of the body. So this is not a prayer of desperation, as a landlord might remind some dodgy tenant to pay his rent, at least half expecting that his reminder will be shredded. This plea brings comfort because it is based upon Covenant. Some people are dead while they live (such as the ungodly widow of 1 Tim. 5:6); this man lives while he is as good as dead.

The German pastor Martin Niemoller wrote of the Bible, 'The Bible: what did this book mean to me during the long and weary years of solitary confinement and then for the last four years at Dachau cell-building? The word of God was simply everything to me – comfort and strength, guidance and hope, master of my days and companion of my nights, the bread which kept me from starvation, and the water of life which refreshed my soul. And even more, "solitary confinement" ceased to be solitary.' This word of promise was his comfort in affliction.

And so he holds on to the word of promise in hope. That is, he places his trust in Christ, who is God's 'amen', God's 'yes' to every promise (2 Cor. 1:20).

B. WE TAKE COMFORT FROM THE FUTURE DEFEAT OF THE WICKED (VV. 51, 52).

Verse 51: 'The insolent (whom we first met in v. 21) utterly deride me, but I do not turn away from your instruction' (as they do, v. 53).' He knows what it is to be mocked and laughed at with bitter scorn by those who turn away from the instruction of the LORD. He knows in experience the misery of being excluded from the fellowship of those, perhaps even within the visible church, who have compromised with truth, to be treated as an extremist because of his zeal for God's standards.

And yet he remembers the 'judgments' of the LORD 'from of old'. Verse 52: 'When I remember your judgments from of old, O LORD, I take comfort.' This does not here mean that he remembers the Ten Commandments and takes comfort; for on their own they would provide no comfort for sinners. It means that he remembers the times in history when the LORD has acted in judgment on behalf of his people and against their enemies, whether it be Pharaoh and his chariots, Og King of Bashan, Sihon King of Heshbon, the Midianites, or any of the other rescues in Israel's history. He remembers these past rescues and takes comfort from them because they assure him of the Covenant faithfulness of the LORD and the certainty of future rescue for him too. The wicked who laugh at him now will one day have the smile wiped off their faces. Every little rescue in the past assures me that there will be more little rescues and then one gigantic final rescue. (The expression 'from of old' is the same as 'from everlasting' and appears also in Psalms 25:6; 41:13; 90:2; 93:2; 103:17 and 106:48.)

C. WE SING HIS WORD AND ARE APPALLED AT THOSE WHO TURN FROM IT (VV. 53, 54).

Verse 53: 'Hot indignation seizes me because of the wicked, who turn away from your instruction.'. His response to the wicked and insolent is 'hot indignation'. He is seized with passionate fury. The word is used in Psalm 11:6 of a scorching wind, and in Lamentations 5:10 of the heat of an oven. But it is important to note that his indignation is not because they are hurting him, painful though that is. He is indignant because they 'turn away from your instruction'. He loves the LORD and longs to see him honoured. It fills him with fury to see him dishonoured and his world spoiled with sin. This is like Paul in Athens, who sees a city ('the house of my sojourning') devoted to idols; and his spirit is hotly indignant (Acts 17:16). He is like the zealous Cambridge missionary Henry Martyn, who wrote, 'I could not endure existence if Jesus were not glorified. It would be hell to me.'

He is indignant because he understands that the God who made this world has graciously given written instruction to all who will read, listen, and heed. When people don't listen to it, he is outraged; he is very hot under the collar. And rightly so.

We too need to learn this indignation. So often we think of someone who has no time for God as 'nice' or 'decent', 'really quite good underneath'. And we find it hard really to feel that he or she is in desperate need of justification by faith, that rebellion against God is really so serious, because we don't really feel that God could be angry with him or her. We need to learn that to live in God's world, taking God's good gifts, but turning away from the written instruction God has given, is a personal insult and an outrage against the Creator of the universe. The singer is right to feel hot indignation, and so should we.

And yet alongside his hot indignation, there are songs. Verse 54, 'Your statutes have been my songs in the house of my sojourning.' Because he loves the LORD, he sings with delight of his statutes. He lives in 'the house of my sojourning' (cf. v. 19), a place where he does not finally belong. This 'house' does not just mean 'wherever I happen to live' (as NRSV 'wherever I make my home'), but is another Covenant word. It is the place to which I do not now belong but which I will one day own because it is promised me in the Covenant.

This is what 'sojourning' means in the Old Testament. So in Genesis 17:8 Abraham is promised, 'I will give to you and to your offspring after you the land of your sojourning.' Isaac passes much the same promise on to Jacob (Gen. 28:4). And it is repeated in Exodus 6:4, 'to give them ... the land in which they lived as sojourners.' As the patriarchs travelled around the promised land, they did not belong; and yet they knew

that one day they would. One day the meek will inherit the
earth (Matt. 5:5); one day Abraham's people will inherit the
world (Rom. 4:13); but not yet. 'The house of my sojourning'
is the house I will one day own. God's statutes are our songs
not because we simply say we don't belong in this world, but
because, although we do not belong in this age, one day we will.
We will own and rule it.

But although that sojourning is in some ways a place of
tears, it is also a place where he can sing because of the word of
the God he loves. And so he sets before us a tension of Christian
experience. On the one hand, a deep hot indignation at the
wicked; on the other, a song-filled delight in the word.

D. In the darkness we remember the blessing of being a believer (vv. 55, 56).

The songs of verse 54 can lighten the darkest night. He remembers, verse 55, the 'name', the Covenant name, the character,
the pledged promises of the Lord 'in the night,' in the times of
darkness and fear. He loves this 'name' (v. 132). In this land of
sojourning, this land travelled through in hope, my song is not
in present blessing but in future hope. 'Your statutes have been
my songs.' Believers have always sung. We sing because we must
somehow find expression for the deep wells of feeling aroused
in our hearts by the word of God.

Sometimes those songs will be laments, it is true. But often
they will be songs of joy in the midst of suffering. The context
of these verses reminds us that we do not sing our hymns and
songs because the present is easy or prosperous; we sing because
the future is glorious, because the word of God assures us of
this.

And so, in response to these gracious promises, I 'keep your
instruction.' And he realizes that keeping the law in his heart
is a blessing given to him by grace: verse 56, 'This blessing has
fallen to me, that I have kept your precepts.'

Comfort and Songs in the Night (vv. 49-56)

It is not clear whether verse 56 means that the keeping of the precepts is itself the blessing (as I have translated), or that the blessing comes because the precepts have been kept (as NIV implies). I think the former is more likely, that in the actual keeping of the precepts, in walking this way, there is blessing, simply because it means walking with the God we love (cf. Ps. 19:11b, 'in keeping them there is great reward').

In some ways this section is a pointer to Christian prayer. The double direction of 'remember' contains within it a theology of prayer. I call upon the LORD to remember his word; and I myself remember his word. As I call upon him to act, and he reminds me that he has promised to act, so he allows himself to be moved to do what he has promised to do; and I myself am given comfort and hope in my affliction. That kind of Bible-soaked prayer can change night-time into song.

PERSONAL RESPONSE QUESTIONS

1. How in practice can you train yourself to remember God's name and his judgments when you are under pressure?

2. How does this remembering by us enable us to pray, calling on him to remember and act on his promises?

8

Section 8:
The Sufficiency of Covenant Love
(vv. 57-64)

Heth

[57]The LORD is my portion;
    I promise to keep your *words*.
[58]I entreat your favour with all my heart;
    be gracious to me according to your *promise*.

[59]When I think on my ways,
    I turn my feet to your *testimonies*;
[60]I hasten and do not delay
    to keep your *commandments*.

[61]Though the cords of the wicked ensnare me,
    I do not forget your *instruction*.
[62]At midnight I rise to praise you,
    because of your righteous *judgments*.

[63]I am a companion of all who fear you,
    of those who keep your *precepts*.
[64]The earth, O LORD, is full of your steadfast love;
    teach me your *statutes*!

Sections 7 and 8 are linked both by the repetition of 'the wicked' (vv. 53, 61) and the theme of singing in the night (vv. 54f, 62). In Section 8 there is an emphasis on the determination of the singer to 'keep' God's word (vv. 57, 60, 63). Although the word 'comfort' is not repeated from Section 7, notice how this section is bracketed by affirmations about the sufficiency and loving sovereignty of the LORD. He is 'my portion' in verse 57; and in verse 64 the whole earth is 'full of your steadfast love'. So the theme is this: the sufficient sovereignty of the LORD motivates the believer to keep God's word. We may take the structure as two pairs of couplets.

A. THE SUFFICIENCY OF GOD MAKES US ZEALOUS TO KEEP HIS WORD (VV. 57-60).

Verse 57: 'The LORD is my portion' (cf. Ps. 16:5; 73:26; 142:5). The word 'portion' refers literally to a portion of territory in the promised land. When the people of Israel entered the promised land, all the tribes were allocated portions of land, except the tribe of Levi. The Levites had no land, but the LORD was their 'portion' (e.g. Num. 18:20; Deut. 10:9; Josh. 13:14). The Levites were a visible sign in the people of God that the promised land was not itself the final destination of the people of God (Heb. 4:1-11), which is why it is such a tragic mistake to think that that land in the Middle East is finally the promise of God.

The presence of the Levites reminded everybody that the promised rest was to be found finally only with the immediate presence of the LORD in the new creation, when believers join him in his eternal seventh day Sabbath rest. Therefore to affirm, 'the LORD is my portion,' is to say I believe his promise. He is all I need, because he is faithful and promises me the land on which I will one day live. This is not saying that I don't care about having a share in the promised land; rather it is to say that one day I will. And therefore I rest all my security in the one who promises me this future. As one paraphrase puts it, 'You are all I want, Lord.' This section breathes the air of love and answering love.

The Sufficiency of Covenant Love (vv. 57-64)

This is no legalistic mentality or obsession with the written word for its own sake, as is clear from the cry, 'The LORD is my portion'. This believer has chosen the LORD, and is satisfied wholly in the LORD he has chosen. He – and he alone – is his portion, his lot, his sufficiency in life and in eternity.

As the hymn-writer John Newton put it:

Precious Bible! what a treasure
Does the Word of God afford!
All I want for life or pleasure
Food and medicine, shield and sword;
Let the world account me poor
Christ and this, I need no more.

In verses 57-60 the singer's zeal is driven by this conviction that the LORD is all he needs. He really believes the LORD is sufficient (his 'portion') for all his needs, circumstances and challenges. This moves him in verse 57b to reaffirm his determination to keep the LORD's words. 'I promise to keep your words.' Notice how in verse 58 the commitment of verse 57b ('I promise to keep ...') is only possible in an atmosphere of prayerful dependence upon grace: Verse 58: 'I entreat your favour with all my heart; be gracious to me according to your promise.'

Verses 59, 60: 'When I think on my ways, I turn my feet to your testimonies; I hasten and do not delay to keep your commandments.' There is an eagerness here, which builds on the promise of verse 57b ('I promise to keep ...'). He lives a reflective life. He thinks on his ways and he considers his path. He evaluates his priorities; he is proactive in taking control of his diary; he thinks ahead what he wants to do with his money, his energies, his gifts and talents. And every time he does this evaluation, he is moved to repentance, to turn his feet to the testimonies of God. And he does this with eagerness; he hastens and does not delay. He does not linger as Lot's wife did, turning back to gaze longingly at the worldly life he is leaving behind (Gen. 19:26). The word 'delay' is an unusual word, also used in Exodus 12:39 for the opposite of the haste with which the people of Israel had to leave Egypt. To repent and turn from sin is to be done with the same urgency and haste with which the people fled from slavery in Egypt.

The story is told of the devil briefing his junior devils. 'Who is going to come up with a good strategy to stop the enemy winning people into his kingdom?' he asked. One devil piped up, 'I'm going to tell them there is no God.' 'That's not a very good strategy,' replied the devil, 'because there is masses of evidence that there is a God. Very few people will really believe you. Anyone else got any ideas?' Someone else said, 'I'm going to tell them there's no judgment.' 'That's a better strategy,' replied the devil. 'But actually men and women know there is accountability. They know that actions have consequences. And so it's still not a very good strategy. Anyone else got any ideas?' And then one demon piped up, 'I'm going to tell them that there's no hurry.' 'Ah,' said the devil, 'that is exactly what you ought to do. That is the perfect strategy.'

Whether you are a Christian or not, we ought to be challenged by verses 59, 60 to turn our feet today, to hasten and not delay to repent, to commit ourselves afresh to turn our ways to his ways. Notice how daily repentance includes both a direction (turning the feet back into the way) and a determination (making haste and not delaying). Both this direction and this determination are driven and motivated by the conviction that the LORD is all we need.

B. WE SHARE THIS ZEAL WITH OTHERS WHO BELIEVE THAT ALL THE WORLD BELONGS TO GOD (vv. 61-64).

We are introduced now to the social implications of the believer's zeal for the LORD. We see the believer in his relations first to 'the wicked' in verse 61, and then to 'all who fear you' in verse 63.

On the one hand (v. 61) he finds himself ensnared and imprisoned in 'the cords of the wicked', the many ways in which those who care nothing for God's instruction seek to frighten and inhibit believers. Their cords are frightening, like the spiders webs in Mirkwood in Tolkein's *The Hobbit*. He cannot escape on his own.

The need for urgent response to the word of God (v. 60) is given fresh sharpness by this context of hostility. Verse 61, 'The cords of the wicked' ensnare him (cf. Ps. 140:5). He is surrounded by people who don't care about God, and he is ensnared by them. They ensnare us in the way we use our time and our money. It is hard as a Christian to do stupid things with our time, in the eyes of the world, and foolish things with our money. It makes no sense to the non-Christian to make costly sacrifices of time to serve in leading a children's group in church, or to help with a summer Christian activity, for example. To do these things is to break out of the cords of the wicked.

It is the same with the stupidity of giving. In the eyes of the world serious and significant Christian giving, giving which really impacts and constrains our lifestyles, does seem very stupid. Once you've given it you can't get it back. Someone gives us an inheritance, and we decide to give all or a large slice of it to the work of Christ in the world. The non-Christian thinks that is daft. How do we know we will not be made redundant next month, and then we will need it? We don't. This kind of sacrificial giving only makes sense if we really believe in the sufficiency of the invisible God. To do these really distinctive Christian things is a breaking free from the cords of the wicked. And only the sufficiency of God will move him to do this, and not to 'forget your instruction.'

His heart, like our hearts, needs reminding of this sufficiency in the night, the time of doubt and anxiety. This is why, I think, he rises 'at midnight ... to praise you because of your righteous judgments.' In the middle of the night, when fears crowd in, he engages in the discipline of conscious praise and so reminds himself of the righteous way God runs the world, and therefore of his safety.

So, on the one hand, there is this external hostility. We have seen this before, and we will see it again. But on the other hand, he is not alone on God's side. Verse 63: 'I am a companion of all who fear you, of those who keep your precepts.' He is surrounded not just by the wicked, but also by others who fear the LORD. This sounds a new note in the psalm. So far the only plural has been the enemies. We have met one believer, one God, and many enemies.

It would however be a great mistake to allow this psalm to re-inforce our Western individualism, our dominant understanding of Christianity as a matter of individual faith and the individual's walk with God. For discipleship always and inevitably expresses itself in companionship, a joyful fellowship, with 'all who fear you' and 'keep your precepts' (v. 63). To these he is a companion, which has the idea of being knit together with them, united with them in a common loyalty and love. It is not, 'I alone hated by a hostile world', but rather, 'we together hated by a hostile world'.

The plural subject of 'keep' in verse 63 ('those who keep ...') balances the singular subject in verses 57, 60 ('I ... keep'). The danger with wholehearted zeal is that I kid myself into believing with Elijah that 'I, and I only, am left' (1 Kings 19:10, 14). This is never so. Always there are others who have not bowed the knee (1 Kings 19:18). When Paul faced hostility in Corinth the Lord Jesus said to him (Acts 18:10), 'Do not be afraid ... for I have many people in this city.' We will see this theme developed in section 10.

But the moment we think of the world as divided into those who fear the LORD and 'the wicked', there is a danger. This danger is that we allow the world's hostility to engender in us a ghetto mentality, in which we circle the wagons, look inwards, enjoy sweet companionship with those who fear the LORD, but practically restrict the sovereignty of God to our circle of believers. That is, we think and act as if the LORD were only actually in control of our little ghetto, and has no power in the wide world outside.

Verse 64 is one of the indicators in this psalm of a healthy doctrine of creation underlying the doctrine of scripture: 'The earth, O LORD, is full of your steadfast love' We shall see this

The Sufficiency of Covenant Love (vv. 57-64)

theme developed in Section 12. To claim that 'The earth ... is full of your steadfast (Covenant) love' is similar to the angels' message that 'the whole earth is full of his glory' (Isa. 6:3). That is, there is no corner of the universe where his people can possibly be beyond his Covenant faithfulness, steadfast love, and care. Even though it does not always look like it, there is no God-forsaken square metre on earth. When he promises the earth to the meek who trust in him, he is not promising more than he can deliver; for the whole earth is his.

Even though the earth contains many wicked who are hostile to those who fear the LORD, it is not possible for a believer to be in any part of the created order which is not full of the LORD's steadfast love. A superstitious farmer may leave a corner of his field for the devil. We fear that God has left some corner of creation for the devil. He has not. He leaves not the tiniest speck of Created Order for the devil. Every part is filled with his steadfast Covenant love to his people. I may go as high as I like or as low as I like but still you are there beside me (Ps. 139).

So this section is the first indication this is not just a solitary psalm. It is sung by a believer who finds himself knit together in fellowship with other believers, united in Covenant love, and pressed together by a hostile world. And yet this is always and everywhere a world that remains full of the steadfast love of the LORD. It is finally a safe world with no corner given over to the devil.

So the theme of this section is the utter sufficiency of God, that he is our 'portion', that the whole earth 'is full of (his) steadfast love.' This sufficiency is the motivation we need to determine to repent and believe afresh today, to turn our steps, to hasten and not delay.

This is a word to those of us who teach the Bible. We want to motivate our hearers to prompt and zealous obedience. We are tempted to beat people over the head with vigorous exhortation; and our hearers may just go away feeling guilty. But in fact the best way to motivate is to spread before them the gracious sufficiency of God.

Personal Response Questions

1. In what areas of your life or relationships do you especially need to remember that the whole earth is full of the Lord's steadfast Covenant love to his people? Where does this not feel as if it is true? How can you pray verses 57 and 64 in that area?

2. Does a strong awareness of the sufficiency of God motivate you to urgent wholehearted discipleship in any particular area of your life at the moment?

9

Section 9:
The Adversity Gospel
(vv. 65-72)

Teth

[65]Well you have dealt with your servant,
O Lᴏʀᴅ, according to your *word*.
[66]Good judgment and knowledge teach me,
for I believe in your *commandments*.

[67]Before I was afflicted I went astray,
but now I keep your *promise*.
[68]Good you are and you do good;
teach me your *statutes*.

[69]The insolent smear me with lies,
but I with my whole heart keep your *precepts*;
[70]their heart is unfeeling like fat,
but I delight in your *instruction*.

[71]Good for me that I was afflicted,
that I might learn your *statutes*.
[72]Good for me the *instruction* of your mouth
more than thousands of gold and silver pieces.

We reach now a most important section. We will call it 'The Adversity Gospel', which is the antidote to the so-called 'prosperity gospel' (which is no gospel). The 'prosperity gospel' is endemic in Christianity all around the world. In one form or another this teaches that if you become a Christian, God wants to bless you and therefore your bank statement will become fatter, your house will get bigger, your car will get faster, your wife will get prettier or your husband more handsome, your children will get cleverer, your health will get better, and all will be for the best in this best of all possible religions. That is to say, things will necessarily get better in this life.

So far in the psalm two tunes or themes have played. One is the delight the singer has in the word of God because it promises him a glorious future. The other is the theme of suffering. He is 'a sojourner' (v. 19), suffering 'scorn and contempt' (v. 22), with princes plotting against him (v. 23), his soul clinging to the dust (v. 25), being taunted (v. 42), and yet with a measure of comfort in affliction (v. 50).

Now in this section the singer does something hugely significant. He plays both tunes together, and shows us how they harmonize. The theme of the section is this: the affliction God gives is his good gift to his people. He gives affliction as his good gift to his people to draw us into, and keep us in, the word. He shows his goodness by allowing his servant to be afflicted by those who care nothing for his word, so that his servant will learn to keep and treasure his word. The process whereby the lover of God's word is afflicted is used by God to deepen that same love. It is not that we have to get through the affliction, and then we will get the good gift later. The affliction itself is paradoxically the good gift of God. This is a process at the heart of the Christian life and one we neglect or despise to our peril.

The key word for this section is 'good'. The Hebrew word family that includes 'good', 'better', 'best', and 'do good' all begin with *teth*. The singer begins five of the eight verses with this word (vv. 65, 66, 68, 71, 72). He also adds in another one later in verse 68 for good measure, to show he is not grudging about this theme of goodness; he is not just putting in the goodness because he needs the Hebrew letter! He is thrilled and taken up with the sheer goodness of God shown towards him.

But how has God been good? That is the surprise.

The section is carefully structured to show what it means. Verses 65-68 go together, bracketed by references to the LORD doing good (65, 68). Then verses 69, 70 are in parallel, contrasting 'they' who are wicked, with 'I' who am righteous by faith. Finally verses 71, 72 are tied together by the same start 'Good/better for me ...'.

A. AFFLICTION IS GOD'S GOOD SCHOOL FOR HIS PEOPLE (vv. 65-68).

He begins with an affirmation. 'Well you have dealt' (NIV request, 'Do good to ...' is misleading here) 'with your servant' (the Covenant relationship word), 'O LORD' (the Covenant God), 'according to your word' (the word of Covenant promise). You have committed yourself to be 'for me' (Rom. 8:31), to be my God, and therefore to bring me good and blessing. Your word says you will do that. And it is my testimony that you have kept your word.

Notice that God's goodness is not a general benevolence, a grandfatherly smile, but rather a goodness according to his word. His goodness consists in keeping the word of his promise. God's promises are like the conduit pipes through which the benefits of God flow to us (Calvin). As Calvin wisely points out, 'we can hope for nothing at his hand until he first bring himself under obligation to us by his word.' Commenting on verse 58, Calvin put it even more strikingly when he wrote, 'that God, in all his promises, is set before us as if he were our willing debtor.' And he has done this in Christ, who is the 'Amen' to every promise (2 Cor. 1:20), the proof he has and will keep them all.

Because he has tasted the goodness of God, he longs for more, not meaning by that a comfortable life, but rather an inward change of life for the better. 'Good judgment' (literally 'taste', which is an acquired taste, for it is not natural to have a taste for moral goodness) 'and knowledge teach me for I believe in your commandments.' He has begun to taste 'the goodness of the word of God' (Heb. 6:5); he is developing a taste for the promises and word of God. His powers or faculties of discernment have been trained to distinguish good from evil (Heb. 5:14). And so he prays for a growing taste for moral goodness. He prays to be taught good judgment, not good head knowledge but a good heart, a good walk from a good heart.

His desire, his prayer here, to be given good taste, good judgment, good knowledge, has been aroused by the good word of promise. One of the marks of convertedness is a growing taste for moral goodness. Notice that goodness in blessing is inseparable from goodness in morality. By contrast, in our culture, 'the good life' generally has very little to do with goodness, and much more to do with pleasure.

But how has the LORD been good? How has he been keeping his Covenant promise to this young believer? How has he aroused in him a taste, a desire, an appetite, for goodness?

The answer is by affliction. Verse 67, 'Before I was afflicted', humbled, brought low, chastened, 'I went astray, but now I keep your promise.' That in a nutshell is my story. When all was easy, success after success, comfort, pleasure, I went astray. Like Ephraim in Jeremiah 31:18, I was like an untrained calf. Or we might say an untrained dog. But now if you want to summarise the direction of my life, it is not arrogant to say that 'I keep your promise.' This is not a perfectionist claim. He means, 'You have made me faithful, you have made me cling to you, by affliction. And now my direction of life is a keeping of your word.'

It is one of the highest marks of the love of the Father that he afflicts his child with pain. Sometimes he does this by financial distress, pressures, or poverty. Sometimes he afflicts by shame, as some moral failure brings upon us public embarrassment or shame. Sometimes affliction comes through illness, sometimes by troubles in the family, sometimes by sheer exhaustion and pressure of work. In a hundred different ways the loving Father afflicts his child that the child may come back to him.

Before this believer was afflicted (which in the context of this psalm means being persecuted for loyalty to God's word), he committed error; his life was off track, not wholeheartedly going God's way and the way of his word. But now, paradoxically now that he is afflicted for loyalty to God's word, he keeps that word.

It is precisely in making an open and costly stand as believers that our hearts are properly orientated and fortified to keep the word for which we suffer. This is a paradox. We might have thought that suffering for the word would incline us to soften our loyalty to the word, to make it a secretive or compromised loyalty. But in the real believer, suffering for the word simply strengthens the determination of the believer to keep that word.

Christian and non-Christian alike have recognized that adversity has its uses. Shakespeare famously put it like this,

> Sweet are the uses of adversity,
> Which, like a toad, ugly and venomous,
> Wears yet a precious jewel in his head.

> (*As you like it*, II.1)

William Cowper was an eighteenth-century poet and hymn-writer who suffered chronic depressive illness both before and after his conversion to Christ. In a moving and all-too-autobiographical poem about a castaway he wrote,

> There is mercy in every place,
> and mercy, encouraging thought!
> Gives even affliction a grace
> And reconciles man to his lot.

When he was in the far country the younger son in Jesus' parable in Luke 15 discovered the emptiness of living for self. But God had his hand on him for good even there. Affliction is like the electric fence put by the caring farmer around his sheep; it gives them pain, but it keeps them safe because it keeps them from wandering. Affliction is the most practical evidence that the Father wills us to walk in his way. If he did not will this, he would not afflict. For 'he does not willingly afflict or grieve the children of men' (Lam. 3:33).

And (v. 68) it is precisely because the singer has been afflicted that he can testify, 'Good you are and you do good'. On that basis of the proven goodness of the LORD he prays again, 'teach me your statutes.' That is, go on afflicting me whenever and wherever necessary to keep me walking your way. Teach me, train me, mentor me, to walk in your statutes. Because if you don't afflict me, I will never learn.

How does this logic work? It is not that affliction improves the intellect or sharpens the concentration. Very often it does the opposite, and leaves us feeling numb and empty. Rather, it is that affliction from the world brings deeply home to me where I do and do not belong. When the world is nice to me, I drift into thinking how good it would be to belong to that nice comfortable flattering world. John Berridge, an eighteenth-century minister in Bedfordshire, wrote, 'A Christian never falls asleep in the fire or in the water, but grows drowsy in the meantime ... we scarcely know how to turn our backs on admiration, though it comes from the vain world; yet a kick from the world does believers less harm than a kiss.' When the world kicks me, then I know I do not belong to it. Too often we pray for members of our families, that they would be happy. We ought rather to pray that they would be holy. And therefore to pray that as and when necessary they would be afflicted in order that they – and we – might be godly. For I will only really deeply learn to walk the way of the word when the world afflicts me.

There is a virtuous circle at work here. I have some small loyalty to the word. For that small loyalty I suffer. That suffering brings home to me that I belong in the age to come; and it stiffens my resolve to be a more open believer. This leads to more suffering. And the more I suffer, the more deeply I pray for God to teach me and lead me in the way of his statutes.

The Adversity Gospel (vv. 65-72)

This was true in a manner even of the Lord Jesus. Not that he ever went astray. And yet, even though he was the Son, he 'learned obedience through what he suffered' (Heb. 5:8). He was never disobedient. But until he suffered he could not learn obedience. And we too are to learn obedience through suffering.

'Whoever has suffered in the flesh has ceased from sin, so as to live the rest of the time in the flesh no longer for human passions but for the will of God' (1 Pet. 4:1, 2). This cannot mean that those who have suffered have achieved sinless perfection. But when I suffer for being a Christian, there is no point holding on as a Christian if I am only interested in blessing in this life. Then for the first time I begin to learn to direct my life firmly God's way. Before I suffer, my discipleship is necessarily shallow and untested. But when I suffer and persevere, then in a fundamental sense the direction of my life has changed and I have in that sense, 'ceased from sin'.

So suffering is a fundamental mark of the goodness of God in answering the prayer of the believer to walk the way of the word.

B. This affliction comes as the believer is smeared with lies because of his loyalty to truth (vv. 69, 70).

Verses 69 and 70 are closely parallel. In each, we begin with something about 'them', the insolent and unfeeling ones, and continue with a contrast 'but I ...'. First (v. 69a), 'The insolent smear me with lies', with falsehood; they blacken my name. Alternatively it may mean that they forge and make up lies. Either way, it hurts to be misrepresented and attacked without cause, as it hurt the Lord Jesus. By contrast (v. 69b), 'I, with my whole heart, keep your precepts.' They are marked by lies, falsehood, so that what they say is not true. The believer, by contrast, is marked by truth, a whole heart, integrity, so that what I say is what I am, what you see is what you get.

And then verse 70, 'their heart is unfeeling (or gross) like fat'; they are callous, hard, and insensitive to human pain. 'But

I delight in your instruction.' They rejoice in falsehood; that is their game, to smear the righteous with lies. But I rejoice in truth, the truth of your word. I love that word with all my heart.

C. THE MORE WE ARE AFFLICTED, THE MORE WE VALUE THE WORD (VV. 71, 72).

But how does it happen that this believer delights in God's instruction (v. 70)? This is the point: that he would never have become like this had he not been afflicted. Until he was afflicted he went his own way. His life too had been marked by falsehood and pretence. There had been in his life a distinction between his public face and the private reality. (In Japan I am told they even have words dedicated to describing this distinction between the public face – *honne* – and the real heart – *tattenai*). He too had had a conscience seared, calloused, hardened. He too had once been desensitised to human grief. He had wept at his own pain but rejoiced at the weeping of his rivals. He had rejoiced when things went well for him but found it hard to rejoice with the joy of others (cf. Rom. 12:15).

It was 'good for me that I was afflicted' (v. 71). This affliction was a mark of the gracious loving hand of God. Because it has taught him to walk in the way of the statutes of God ('... that I might learn your statutes' v. 71). This is like the wilderness training of Israel, done by God, 'that he might humble you and test you, to do you good in the end' (Deut. 8:16). 'He softens our natural hardness by the strokes of a hammer' (Calvin). This also was the testimony of King Hezekiah after his illness, in Isaiah 38:17, 'Behold, it was for my welfare that I had great bitterness.' It was the testimony of Deuteronomy 8:16, which says of the wilderness that the LORD did it, 'that he might humble you and test you, to do you good in the end.'

Affliction for the word makes me more loyal than ever to the word. This is true in Christian experience. It is only as we experience the public toughness of standing for the word of

The Adversity Gospel (vv. 65-72)

God in a hostile environment that scripture itself comes alive in our understanding and experience. And as it comes alive in this context of suffering, so we begin to grasp just how very great and precious are the promises of the word of God (2 Pet. 1:4).

Because of that goodness of God, verse 72 is true: 'Good for me the instruction of your mouth, more than thousands of gold and silver pieces.' To call scripture 'the instruction of your mouth' is very personal. These are the words that sprang from your beloved lips. It is like the old advertisements for HMV, that show a dog listening to the gramophone trumpet, because he hears there a perfect reproduction of 'His Master's Voice'. So in scripture we hear as it were, a recording of the very voice of God.

Why is the instruction of his mouth so valuable to me? Because I was afflicted. And when I was afflicted the message finally got through to my heart and body that I do not belong in this age; I belong to the age to come. And the only sure tie between me and the age to come is the instruction of his mouth, his Covenant word. As the city I was building for myself crumbled and collapsed, I realized I needed to seek a better city (Heb. 11:10).

And so we have here a deep truth. No man will love his Bible until God has afflicted him. He may be intrigued by it. He may have an intellectual affection for it. He may have been brought up to have a cultural affinity with it, or an aesthetic love of its verbal resonances. But he will not delight in that word above all the wealth of the world until he has been afflicted, until he has felt the fragility of this world, this age, this mortal body. But when that happens he will cling to the word as the only tie to the age to come. Like a falling mountaineer clinging to his rope, he knows that the word of God is the only tie to safety.

PERSONAL RESPONSE QUESTIONS

1. Is there a time in your life before you were a Christian when life was mainly quite easy? How did God change that?

2. Can you sing verses 67 and 71? Since you became a Christian, is there an experience of affliction that you can now see was God's goodness to you?

10

Section 10:
Affliction and Fellowship
(vv. 73-80)

Yodh

[73]Your hands have made and fashioned me;
   give me understanding that I may learn your *commandments*.
[74]Those who fear you shall see me and rejoice,
   because I have hoped in your *word*.
[75]I know, O Lord, that your *judgments* are righteous,
   and that in faithfulness you have afflicted me.
[76]Let your steadfast love comfort me
   according to your *promise* to your servant.

[77]Let your mercy come to me, that I may live;
   for your *instruction* is my delight.
[78]Let the insolent be put to shame, because they have
   wronged me with falsehood;
   as for me, I will meditate on your *precepts*.
[79]Let those who fear you turn to me,
   that they may know your *testimonies*.
[80]May my heart be blameless in your *statutes*,
   that I may not be put to shame!

As afflicted believers we are encouraged by other afflicted believers

The theme of affliction continues from Section 9 (see v. 75), and the theme of comfort reappears in verse 76. Within the section there is a double reference to 'shame' in verses 78, 80. But perhaps the most significant feature is the repeated reference to 'those who fear you' in verses 74, 79. This picks up the first reference to other believers back in verse 63 and suggests that fellowship is a significant theme here.

We may perhaps say fancifully that in Satan's armoury there is a missile labelled I-I-O. Satan has written beside it instructions for his junior devils. The instructions read, 'Sometimes our battle will be going badly. A man or woman will follow our Enemy wholeheartedly. We will ask permission to attack him with loss, bereavement, disaster or sickness, as we did with Job. That permission will be granted, and we will have fun giving him a thoroughly miserable time. Usually that will do the trick, and prove that he is not really a believer, and he will tumble back into our camp. But sometimes the wretch will obstinately insist on continuing to follow our Enemy.'

'Under those circumstances try launching the I-I-O missile at him. The letters stand for, "I, and I Only am left, and they seek my life also". This missile will generally get right through to our subject's heart. Persuade him that it's not just that he is having a tough time, but that he is all alone. That will really get to him. I used it on that wretched prophet Elijah and it would have worked wonders if our Enemy hadn't intervened personally, which seemed to me very unfair' (cf. 1 Kings 19:10).

In Section 9 we saw the deep goodness with which the LORD afflicts his servant, to keep him walking in the way. This psalm seems for the most part a very individual one: just me and my God. Until verse 63 the only plural is the enemies (e.g. vv. 21-23), of whom there seem to be plenty. But we saw in verse 63 that there are others who fear God, and the singer is their companion. This theme of fellowship is now developed.

Affliction and Fellowship (vv. 73-80)

This section is about the encouraging example of the suffering and vindicated believer.

In his affliction he is very aware that God has made him, and God is dealing with him. He is like clay in the hands of the potter. Verse 73, 'Your hands have made and fashioned me', literally, 'firmed me', shaped me. He has been shaped not just in the womb, but shaped also by affliction. God is at work in him and on him. And so he prays, verse 73b, 'give me understanding that I may learn your commandments.' That is, please work on me not just from the outside, but work in me, to give understanding in my heart, to grant me wisdom in the inmost parts, that I may learn to walk the way of your commandments. He is very conscious of the active loving hand of God on his life.

And then in verse 74 he looks around. 'Those who fear you' – my fellow believers – 'shall see me and rejoice, because I have hoped in your word.' When they see me, afflicted but trusting, hurting and hoping, holding on to your word of promise, they too will rejoice and take courage.

This is the positive impact of a suffering believer. Here is the encouragement when the visible world shouts at me that it is stupid to trust the word of God about the invisible age to come. It makes such an impact to see another visible, audible, tangible human being who really thinks the written word of God is more trustworthy than the sensible (oh, so sensible!) evidence of the world. It is wonderful to see someone else who really believes God means what he says, and proves he believes it by sticking to God when there's nothing in it for him. The believer in the Adversity Gospel is a powerful encouragement to others, much more powerful than the temporarily prosperous pseudo-believer in the 'prosperity gospel'. When I see the complacent comfort of the prosperity believer, I just become envious or I despair; but when I see the living faith of the adversity believer, I am deeply encouraged to persevere myself.

I wonder how you react when you read some wonderful testimony of God's miraculous help in somebody's life. Perhaps you hear a testimony of a childless couple who prayed and now have a child, or the story of a man made redundant who prayed and now has a wonderful job. I went to a Christian conference where it was all like that. All the stories we heard were like that. I hope I was pleased for them, that I rejoiced with them. I hope I joined them in thanking God for his mercy on them. But to be quite honest I was not nearly so encouraged in my struggles as when I see a believer who is really going through hard times, and yet still holding on to the word of God.

It is good to hear of answers to prayer that change circumstances. But it is better to hear of answers to prayer that change people, so that they persevere in unchanged circumstances. I hope it is not perverse of me to hope to hear a testimony more like this: 'My wife was seriously ill. We prayed for her healing. But she died. And I am still trusting the faithfulness and promises of God.' Or, 'We longed for a child. And God has chosen not to give us a child. But we are still trusting the faithfulness of God.' Or, 'I prayed for a job. And I haven't got a job. But I am still trusting.'

'Those who fear you will see me', the afflicted believer who believes the Adversity Gospel, suffering, smeared with lies, oppressed by powerful enemies, and they will 'rejoice' not because my affliction has ended (because it hasn't) but 'because I have hoped in your word.' And that encourages them too to hope in your word.

To the extent to which our lives are comfortable and easy, we are on the fringes of the worldwide church. Because the same kinds of suffering are being experienced by the fellowship of believers all through the world (1 Pet. 5:9). A believer who holds on in the tough times is a signpost to the future.

No Israelites grumbled when they left Egypt. No Israelites grumbled when they crossed the Red Sea. No Israelites grumbled when water flowed from the rock and manna fell from heaven. You don't need faith to praise under those circumstances (Exod. 15–17). But you need faith to hold on when suffering, when facing a seemingly uncrossable sea with enemies behind, when walking through a desert with seemingly no water. It needs faith to believe in Christ who is the rock from which the water will pour in God's good time (1 Cor. 10:4).

Sometimes we may be worried because we are not being afflicted. Is it a sign that there is something wrong with our Christian lives? I take it we must not be silly about this, as it were carrying around with us our bundle of sticks ready to be burnt at the stake. When we experience good times, let us be thankful and generous with the blessings we enjoy (cf. 1 Tim. 6:17-19). But let us remember that the normal Christian life is affliction. By nature we are relaxed when all is good, and surprised when things go wrong. We ought to be the reverse: when things are tough, we should say to ourselves, 'Another normal day in the Christian life,' but when they go well we should exclaim with surprise, 'How odd! I am not being afflicted.'

The suffering and afflicted believer is an inspiration to others undergoing trials. This is precisely the incentive given to struggling Christians by the writer of the letter to the Hebrews. When he wants to encourage them in tough times he writes, 'Consider him who endured from sinners such hostility against himself (that is, Jesus the adversity believer), so that you may not grow weary or fainthearted' (Heb. 12:3). We should see him and rejoice, because he hoped in your word. And his hope was not disappointed. We see on the third day the proof that he did not hope in vain.

We follow the example of one who entrusted himself to him who judges justly (1 Pet. 2:23). And because of Christ we know more fully than our singer ever did, that the judgments of God are righteous (v. 75a, 'I know, O LORD, that your judgments are righteous'), that he does govern the world aright, that he will act to rescue his righteous ones who trust in him. He has always acted to humble the proud and to exalt the humble. We see this pattern, for example, in Hannah's prayer in 1 Samuel 2:1-10.

It follows that when he does afflict his servants, he does so (v. 75b) 'in faithfulness'. Our affliction is the concrete expression in this life of his Covenant faithfulness to us. Were he not faithful to his promise, he would not trouble to afflict me. For he does not willingly afflict; he afflicts because it is the only way to achieve his promise and to keep me walking in his way. He has promised that the saints will persevere; but no saint will ever persevere unless the LORD afflicts him on the way. The affliction is not the failure of God's faithfulness, but precisely the expression of it.

Because he knows this about his affliction he can confidently pray (v. 76), 'Let your steadfast (Covenant) love comfort me according to your promise to your servant.' Affliction is, as it were, the goodness of God's left hand; he does it, but it does not come naturally to him. (If you are left-handed, then feel free to call it the goodness of God's right hand!)

And so as he prays for the mercy of God (v. 77, 'Let your mercy come to me, that I may live'), he knows it will come in God's good time. For every one who delights in the Covenant word (v. 77b) mercy will come. We know that because on the third day it came to the Lord Jesus who entrusted himself to him who judges justly.

The flip side of that mercy must be the shame of the insolent (v. 78). The proud oppressors, who smear him with lies (v. 69) and wrong him with falsehood (v. 78) will finally be brought to shame. They will be publicly exposed as frauds and humbled in the sight of the whole universe.

In his suffering, he knows he needs to meditate on both sides of this truth of salvation and judgment (v. 78c, 'as for me, I will meditate on your precepts'). He knows that when he tosses and turns in the night with a troubled mind, he must meditate not on their falsehoods (writing mental letters of grievance to the newspapers, etc.), but on the precepts and promises of the Covenant God. That will be his meditation.

And as he does that, focusing on the Covenant word, so (v. 79), 'Let those who fear you turn to me, that they may know your testimonies.' Supremely this is fulfilled in the Lord Jesus Christ, as we turn to him. But as we walk in his footsteps, this may be true of us. What happens when Christians turn to us, for example? Do they see in us men or women who hope in the word of God, who walk his way, who in the midst of affliction have our hearts and minds filled with his testimonies rather than the lies of the world? When that happens, the effect of our lives on our fellow believers will be that they too will 'know your testimonies', that is know how to walk in them and know that they are true. They will know that all who remain faithful to him will be vindicated on the last day. For the vindication of the believer is the proof of the trustworthiness of the word of God.

Conscious as always of his need for grace he prays (v. 80), 'May my heart be blameless (the prayer of v. 1) in your statutes, that I may not be put to shame.' He prays that the public impact of his life will not be as a fraud exposed, but as a believer unveiled. We ought to develop an appropriate honesty with one another, so that we have some idea of the afflictions and pressures facing one another, and therefore can see something of the inspiring examples of one another's faith.

And so in Sections 9 and 10 we see two stages. First, the loving affliction of the LORD on the believer, to turn him to, and keep him in, the way. And then the outflow of that potter's work, as others who fear the LORD see him and rejoice, turn to him and know to walk the way of the LORD.

This section clearly illustrates the fulfilment of the psalm in the Lord Jesus Christ. He himself is the believer who is afflicted, who is wronged with falsehood, who in his suffering is steadfast in hoping in the promise of God. In his resurrection we see brought forward into human history the final vindication of every believer. The shame heaped on Jesus at Calvary will rebound onto all who have placed him on the Cross, and who hate his followers.

We learn from this section that the life, death and resurrection of Jesus Christ are the pattern of discipleship towards which other disciples should turn, and in which other disciples may rejoice. We too are called to walk this road, maligned yet righteous, faithful under affliction, that we may be sources of encouragement and joy to our fellow believers.

This really is the antidote to the prosperity gospel and it is very necessary. A believer in one East Asian country commented that, 'Usually before people become Christians we just talk about the benefits, the blessings. Only after people become Christians do we talk about the hardships. That's why there are so many weak believers in the churches. And when they meet difficulties they easily fall away, and then it's very difficult to ever win them back.'

A Cornhill student told me that in his country some churches have changed the marriage vows. So that instead of saying 'For better or worse', they say 'For better or best', and instead of saying 'For richer or poorer', they say, 'For richer or richest'. Because, it is argued, life for a Christian couple could not possibly get poorer or worse. This lie will breed a generation of disillusioned men and women who have tried this pseudo-Christianity and mistaken it for the real thing. Because in the real thing, the Adversity Gospel, the LORD proves his goodness by sending affliction, that we may learn to walk together in his ways. It may not look good on our brochures or our church noticeboards ('Come here and enter a life of blessed suffering!'), but it is true. May God help us to rejoice in that deep and paradoxical truth.

PERSONAL RESPONSE QUESTIONS

1. In what ways has the suffering example of other Christians, and supremely of the Lord Jesus Christ, encouraged you and made you rejoice?

2. Do you know whether others can say the same about you?

11

Section 11:
Waiting in Urgent Hope
(vv. 81-88)

Kaph

[81]It longs, my soul, for your salvation;
  I hope in your *word*.
[82]They long, my eyes, for your *promise*;
  I ask, 'When will you comfort me?'

[83]For I have become like a wineskin in the smoke,
  yet I have not forgotten your *statutes*.
[84]How long must your servant endure?
  When will you pass *judgment* on those who persecute me?

[85]The insolent have dug pitfalls for me;
  they do not live according to your *instruction*.
[86]All your *commandments* are sure;
  they persecute me with falsehood; help me!

[87]They have almost made an end of me on earth,
  but I have not forsaken your *precepts*.
[88]In your steadfast love give me life,
  that I may keep the *testimonies* of your mouth.

At the end of Section 10 we could almost be forgiven for feeling a bit upbeat. The singer knows the LORD's hand is on him for good. And he knows that other believers will rejoice as they see him holding on in hope. But now the darkness returns, in a section that is perhaps the most desperate of the psalm. It is not as dark as Job's lament in Job 3, but it is pretty painful, all the same. Spurgeon calls this the midnight of the psalm.

A. THE PLIGHT: REAL BELIEF MEANS A DESPERATE LONGING FOR GOD TO KEEP HIS PROMISE (vv. 81-84).

Verses 81 and 82 are closely parallel. Each begins with the verb 'to long' (which begins with *kaph*). Verse 81, 'It longs, my soul' (that is, my life, my self); that is perhaps a bit weak. It is that my soul is exhausted with longing, it faints with longing (AV 'my soul fainteth'), I long with all my heart, I feel exhausted, played out, worn down, ground down into the dust (it's the same word used in verse 87 for 'made an end of'). It 'longs ... for your salvation', your future rescue; 'I hope in your word', but that's all I've got to go on. There doesn't seem to be much evidence here in this life of your future rescue. And so I just hope in your word. (The object of hope in this psalm is always the word of God.)

On the one hand there is the real subjective experience of utter exhaustion with grief; and on the other the sure and certain hope of the word of promise. He longs, that is, for Christ, who is the "Amen" to all the promises of God. But it is a deep longing, as is emphasized again in verse 82, 'They long, my eyes,' they fail, they grow dim with looking for something that hasn't come, as hope deferred makes the heart sick (Prov. 13:12) 'for your promise; I ask, "When will you comfort me?" ' How long, O LORD? Spurgeon speaks of heaven being taken by storm with the artillery of tears. The eye is the window of the soul; and these eyes are tired, sad, and weakened by grief. This longing is not spiritual in some Greek unbodily way, but rather bodily and visceral.

Waiting in Urgent Hope (vv. 81-88)

Because, verse 83a, 'I have become like a wineskin in the smoke,' like the dried up cracked wineskins of the men of Gibeon in Joshua 9:4. Like Job (Job 16:8) he has been shrivelled up; his skin turns black and falls from him (Job 30:30). He is, quite literally, burnt out, wasted by suffering. You can see it in his eyes. He has a lined face, a furrowed brow, sunken eyes, emaciated skin, and visible bones. This is an intense and lingering affliction.

And 'yet', verse 83b, 'I have not forgotten your statutes.' Still he holds on to the Covenant word.

But as he does he cries out, verse 84, 'How long must your servant endure?' (literally, 'how many the days of your servant?') 'When will you pass judgment on those who persecute me?' He prays for this judgment because this judgment at last will be just and fair.

This verse reminds us that there are two sides to the last judgment, and they are inseparable. The people of God will not have salvation until the enemies of God are judged. That is why we long for the end of the world and pray, 'Your kingdom come'.

This painful picture of the deeply suffering believer watching and looking with his whole being for the rescue promised in the word of God, is the shape of authentic discipleship. Like the widow in Luke 18:1-8, he knows that it is only in the righteous judgments of the LORD that he has any hope. Because God's word is the promise of his righteous kingdom, the singer fixes his hope on that word.

We need to ask whether the shape and tone of our relationship with God reflects this authentic paradigm. Are our Christian lives characterized by longing, waiting, and prayer for his final comfort (v. 82) and therefore his final judgments (v. 84)? Does the prayer 'your kingdom come' trip off our tongues unthinkingly, or is it wrung out of us by the pressure of otherwise unbearable suffering?

B. The persecutors: to stray from the instruction of God means to be hostile to the people of God (vv. 85-88).

The reference in verse 84b to 'those who persecute me' prompts him to dwell for a while on these people. In verses 85, 86 a new tune begins to be faintly heard, a tune that will sound strongly in the next section. Notice the contrast.

On the one hand, verse 85, 'The insolent have dug pitfalls for me; they do not live according to your instruction.' They go astray, and wherever they go, they dig pits, places of falling (cf. Ps. 57:6). The insolent are hostile to God; and because they are hostile to God, they are hostile to God's people. As Satan's agents, they are dedicated not only to their own ungodliness, but to tripping up God's people, making them stumble (cf. Matt. 18:6). Like Satan in Job, the one thing they cannot abide is the true believer, the man or woman who walks this earth blameless and upright, loving God and turning from evil. This they cannot stand. Nothing pleases them more than seeing a believer come a cropper, go flat on his face. Because this confirms them in the belief they would like to hold, that there is no such thing as a real believer to show them up for who they are (cf. Job 1:8-10). They do this because (v. 85b) they do not live according to the Lord's instruction. And because they do not live this way, they badly want others to follow their example (cf. 1 Pet. 4:4). It makes them feel more comfortable.

But on the other hand, in contrast to these people who cause stumbling, there is something that never causes stumbling. Verse 86, 'All your commandments are sure' – not places of falling, pits, but places of stability, certainty, and steadiness. 'They persecute me with falsehood; help me!'

Verses 87 and 88 take us back to the desperation of the start of the section. Verse 87, 'They have almost made an end of me' (wiped me, consumed me, a different form of the same verb 'to long' in vv. 81, 82) 'on earth, but I (emphatic) have not forsaken your precepts.' There is almost nothing of me left; 'they have almost made an end of me'. But while I may be a shadow of my former self, the 'I' that remains, has not forsaken your precepts. And because you are not the God of the dead but of the living (Matt. 22:32), they will never finally make an end of me. Spurgeon comments nicely that these persecutors, 'could only touch his earthly life and earthly goods. He had an eternal portion which they could not even nibble at.'

If I hold on to the precepts I will be rescued by the promises; for they are the same word. And there is something triumphant about that. The lions are chained (as in Bunyan's imagery in *The Pilgrim's Progress*); they can range no further than God permits.

And so, at the end of the first half of the psalm, he appeals, verse 88, 'In your steadfast (loyal, Covenant) love give me life, that I may keep the testimonies of your mouth.' The word 'steadfast love' comes six times in this psalm; in three of these it is linked to the plea, 'give me life' (here and in vv. 149, 159). He is not praying, 'Because I have been good and faithful, please do your part; you owe me one.' He is praying, 'So far you have upheld me; now continue to uphold me, give me life, that I may continue in this way.'

So, holding the first and second parts of this section together, let us consider both the Plight and the Persecutors. We have a picture of two paths through life. The first is to divert from the instruction of God. When I shift from truth to falsehood I naturally want others to come with me, so as to 'play me onside' morally and make me feel that what I am doing is alright. And so, when I meet a real believer, who will not share my values, I find myself deeply hostile to him or her. I want to smear them with falsehood, and to show that they do not have integrity. Nothing would please me more than for them to stumble. I want to set traps for him.

The second path is to hold on to the sure word of God. When I do this, I must expect this age to be full of painful suffering, and discipleship to be shaped by longing, aching prayer. This prayer will not be just a wishful-thinking desperation; it will be prayer informed and nourished by the Covenant word and promises.

We have now reached the midpoint of the psalm. The singer is desperate, played out; and yet he hopes against hope, and rests his destiny and reputation on the spoken word of God. Even in the darkness he affirms that this word is 'sure' (v. 86). But is it? This is the question he now answers in Section 12, perhaps the most deeply glorious of the whole psalm, with which we begin the second half.

Personal Response Questions

1. What experience do you, or Christians known to you, have of desperate prayer and longing like this section of the psalm?

2. What 'pitfalls' are put in your way to make you fall as a Christian?

[89]Forever, O Lord, your *word*
  is firmly fixed in the heavens.
[90]Your faithfulness endures to all generations;
  you have made firm the earth, and it stands firm.
[91]By your *judgment* they stand firm this day,
  for all things are your servants.
[92]If your *instruction* had not been my delight,
  I would have perished in my affliction.

[93]Forever I will not forget your *precepts*,
  for by them you have given me life.
[94]I am yours; save me,
  for I have sought your *precepts*.
[95]The wicked lie in wait to destroy me,
  but I consider your *testimonies*.
[96]To all all-ness I see a cutting off,
  but wide your *commandment* exceedingly.

Three great words or ideas set the tone for this great section. The first is 'forever'; this is the first word in each half (vv. 89, 93), and marks the section as another four plus four. It also gives it an upbeat triumphant tone. The second is two synonymous words meaning 'firm' or 'firmly fixed' in verse 89, verse 90 (twice) and verse 91. The third is the idea of unlimited extent in verse 96; this is very similar to 'forever', but extending through space as well as time.

Melvin Tinker tells the following story:

> Several years ago the famous economist E. F. Schumacher of the book, 'Small is Beautiful' fame gave a talk in London which began with an account of his recent trip to St. Petersburg, Russia, which then was under communist wraps as Leningrad. Despite having a map in hand which he followed painstakingly, he realized that he was lost.
>
> What he saw on the paper didn't fit with what he saw right in front of his eyes, several huge Russian Orthodox churches. They weren't on the map and yet he was certain he knew which street he was on. 'Ah' said the Soviet tourist guide, trying to be helpful. 'That's simple. We don't show churches on our maps.'
>
> Schumacher went on to say this: 'It then occurred to me that this is not the first time I had been given a map which failed to show things I could see right in front of my eyes. All through school and university I had been given maps of life and knowledge on which there was hardly a trace of many of the things that I most cared about and that seemed to me to be of the greatest possible importance to the conduct of my life.' In other words, what he had been taught at school and college and picked up from the media missed out issues of faith which were so vital to him.

The maps the world shows us do not show the most important things there are. This kind of mismatch unsettles us. And one of the big questions any Christian must face is this: does the map the Bible draws actually correspond to the world in which I live?

In Section 10, I fancifully described a weapon in Satan's armoury. Here is another. He has a huge stockpile of this, which is a kind of nerve gas. It is labelled, 'Agent IOWIC'. And judging by the way it is piled high, it is an important ingredient in Satan's armoury.

Here is Satan briefing his underlings on its use. 'I want to introduce you to a very powerful agent, that has been sprayed widely over western Europe and the USA to great effect. It is a nerve agent that paralyses the nerve of the Enemy's followers most effectively. IOWIC stands for, 'It Only Works In Church'. It operates as follows. When one of the Enemy's disciples is getting really enthusiastic about the Enemy, he sings with all his heart in their meetings; he begins to understand the Enemy's book and love it; he turns from our diabolical ways to the Enemy's way. Then spray him with this, and I will tell you what will happen.

'He will go out from his exciting, moving, enlightening meeting – in church or summer camp or CU. He will go out into the workplace, the non-Christian family, the sports club. And he will find his nerve paralysed by a deep conviction that all these things he has been so excited about *only work in church*. Take him past that top shelf in the newsagents, and as the familiar lusts warm up, this agent will persuade him that all his longings for purity only work in church or at camp. Put him in his boss's office as his boss flatters him and tells him what good prospects he has at work; and as the familiar pride and selfish ambition stir, this agent will convince him that all his feelings when he sang, 'Take my life and let it be, consecrated all to thee ...', all those feelings *only work in church*. But actually these pious things don't really work in the real world outside.'

We have reached the half-way point in Psalm 119. We have had eleven sections, and we have eleven to go. And it seems that this first section of the second half has a particular significance, just as Section 1 set the scene for the whole psalm. We have here vital doctrine, which is God's antidote to Agent IOWIC.

The theme of this important section is the limitless scope and therefore unthreatened security possessed by the one who holds on to the creative word of the Creator God. The theology here is awesome, for it ties the Covenant word of God to the whole Created Order. The world is as it is, because the word is as it is. The word is sure because it is the foundation of the world.

A. THE SECURITY OF THE WHOLE CREATION RESTS ON THE FIRMNESS OF THE WORD OF GOD (vv. 89-92).

Just as the psalm began with three verses of crucial doctrine followed by a verse of response, so the second half begins with three verses of doctrine and then a verse expressing the consequence. Let us consider the doctrine first, in verses 89-91. Verse 89, 'Forever, O LORD, your word is firmly fixed in the heavens.' That is, your word as it were stations itself, stands ready for duty, takes its place, in the heavens. It is the same idea as when the LORD himself takes his place in the chair of the divine council in Psalm 82:1, or when in Proverbs 8:2 wisdom takes her stand at the crossroads. Psalm 33:6 says, 'By the word of the LORD were the heavens made and by the breath of his mouth all their host.' The world was made at the command of the word of God. And the Covenant word of scripture is inseparable from the word of creation. No insolent person can shift the word of God from its place in the heavens. No philosopher proclaiming the death of God can remove it. It stands firmly fixed 'forever'. (The word 'forever', like the word 'steadfast love', is particularly associated with the Covenant in, for example, 1 Chronicles 17:12-14). The word that controls, shapes and fixes the world is the sure forever word of the Covenant. No princes, no powerful people proclaiming that all truth is but a power play, or that might is right, can shift from the heavens the word of God. This is the grand affirmation with which the second half of the psalm opens. You cannot untie the world from the word.

As we explore this practical theology of the word of God, it is important to bear in mind four truths about the Spirit of God. Sometimes a false dichotomy is made between word and Spirit, and we need good theology to correct it. Psalm 33:6

holds the word of the LORD and the 'breath' (or 'Spirit') of the LORD very closely together.

The first truth is that everything God does, he does by his Spirit. The Spirit is, as someone has said, the executive arm of the Godhead. All that God does among his people, he does by his Spirit. Second, scripture does not always signal this truth explicitly. Some parts of scripture speak about the Spirit, and others don't; but always he is there. Psalm 119 doesn't, which is why this exposition of it makes little explicitly of the Spirit; but always he is there. Nothing of this believer's experience would happen were it not for his ministry. Third, although word and Spirit are not identical (the word is not the fourth person of a Quaternity!), they are inseparable. Just as the words that I speak are not the same as the breath that I breathe out as I speak, so with the word and Spirit of God. But, as with breath and words, you cannot separate them. We must not fall into that shallow trap of saying that some people have more Spirit and less word, whereas others have less Spirit and more word. Fourth, I take it that the Spirit of God is at work in this singer in an anticipatory way. He lives under the old Covenant, before the Spirit has been poured out on all believers at Pentecost, to live in them forever. But unless the Spirit of God had been at work upon him he could not believe, let alone delight in the word of God. Nothing good would be going on in him.

This triumphant beginning of this section is a wonderful contrast to the almost dead brother who sings it. In it the fixity of the word stands in contrast to the fragility of the believer who sings of it. For *he* certainly does not stand firmly fixed in heaven. He is very much on earth, in the dust, nearly dead. And yet he holds on to this word firmly fixed in the heavens.

Verse 90 continues this theme. It is one of the four verses noted earlier that have a replacement for the regular eight 'word' words. Here the substitute is 'faithfulness'. 'Your faithfulness (that is the sure steadiness of the Covenant word) endures to all generations (i.e. forever); you have made firm the earth and it stands firm.' The order and stability of the created work of God is guaranteed by the authority of the word of God. And therefore the believer who rests upon that word, rests upon firmness and will not fall into a pit.

And though the earth is, as it were, suspended in the midst of the sea, surrounded by chaos and threat, it is firmly fixed by the word of God. He has spoken his word to bring creation into being. After the Flood he has spoken the word of universal Covenant faithfulness with creation; so this word is not negated or undone by human rebellion, even in very extreme form (Gen. 6:5). It is because of the firmness and faithfulness of the Creator's word that the earth stands firm. Nothing that human beings can do, and nothing that Satan can do, can destroy the good world God has made.

Verse 91, 'By your judgment they stand firm this day, for all things are your servants.' This creation doctrine means that every atom in the universe serves the will and purpose of the Covenant God. There is no backwater of creation, no corner handed over to the devil (as we saw in v. 64), which is outside the sovereignty of the Creator who has spoken his word. (NIV 'Your laws endure to this day' rather misses the point, which is that by the word of God the world stands firm.) The whole world stands to attention, ready for duty, ready to do the bidding of its Creator. By his word of power Christ upholds the universe (Heb. 1:3); in him all things hold together, and he is the source of coherence for the universe (Col. 1:17). We live in a world under siege from evil. But one day that siege will be lifted and the world will emerge into a new age of righteousness, a new heavens and new earth. The creation itself will be set free from its bondage to decay and enjoy at last the freedom of being properly governed by the children of God, as it was always meant to be (Rom. 8:19-21).

In a way these first three verses of the second half mirror the first three verses of the first half. Just as verses 1-3 affirm the blessing to those who walk his way, so verses 89-91 assert that we may walk this way with confidence because it is the way upon which the whole world is built. When we walk this way we do not carve out for ourselves, as some little minority religious grouping, a social order of our own construction. No, we walk along the grain of the universe. And therefore we are safe.

Which is why he goes on in verse 92 with the consequence, 'If your instruction had not been my delight, I would have perished in my affliction.' Plenty do perish in affliction. There is nothing automatically good about affliction. Affliction destroys some, in a descending cycle of bitterness and anger. Only if affliction drives us to delight in the word (vv. 67, 71) does it do us good. So what does he mean by saying that his survival is linked to his delight in the instruction of God?

This verse is not, I think, making a psychological point, that the inward conviction of the singer gives him hope and keeps him alive. This is how Spurgeon reads it here: 'When worn with pain until the brain has become dazed and the reason well-nigh extinguished, a sweet text has whispered to us its heart-cheering assurance, and our poor struggling mind has reposed upon the bosom of God'.

Rather I think the point is that his delight in the word is a mark of a real believer, who is attached by cords of Covenant love to the world as it actually is, to life. The instruction of the Lord is the foundation upon which the world is built. That is to say, our safety does not rest on the subjective up's and down's of experienced Bible delight, as if in the troughs we become less secure and more liable to perish. Rather, our imperfect and variable experience of Bible delight is evidence that we really do walk in Covenant relationship with the God whose word holds firm the world. And therefore this delight assures us of our ultimate safety.

We may therefore be confident that when we commend Christian morality to the wider world, we are not just arguing our corner in the religious marketplace, and trying to persuade people to join our club, with our particular, and arbitrary, rules. Rather we are commending to them living along the grain of the world as it is. Let me give two examples of this.

First, the Sabbath principle. Scripture teaches that the rhythm of work and rest, six days work and one day rest, is not just a religious institution followed by ancient Israel and now abrogated under the New Covenant. It is also in some way hard-wired into the Created Order. This kind of rhythm – it doesn't particularly matter which day, and it's not a matter of rules – but this kind of rhythm is the way we are made. And when the world around us takes pride in the busyness of a 24/7 lifestyle, we need have no shame in commending to them the biblical rhythm. This word of God is the word that is firmly fixed in the heavens.

A distinguished physician wrote to *The Times* in 1991 to say, 'We doctors in the treatment of nervous diseases, are compelled to provide periods of rest. Some of these periods are, I think, only Sundays in arrears.' That is to say, because the world is as the word says, living by the word is actually the best and wisest thing to do. The map the word gives us corresponds to the world as it is. And therefore Christians need not be defensive when commending the standards of God in the public sphere. We can say to them, 'You can do what you like. We are not trying to boss you around or throw our weight around by political machinations. We are simply saying that this word gives the map which describes the world as it is and human beings as we are. And therefore we neglect it to our peril.'

The second example is sex and marriage. Many Christians feel very much on the defensive in the workplace or sports club if we are committed to sexual intimacy only between a man and a woman within the public commitment of marriage. We are regarded as dinosaurs; we feel like dinosaurs. And probably we are tempted to keep quiet when the conversation turns to these subjects. After all, how do we avoid coming across as party-poopers and kill-joys?

The Word and the World (vv. 89-96)

But once we grasp that the 'word' that says sex is for marriage is the word by which the heavens were made, the word that put in place the structure and order of the universe, that what we are living by are not local rules for our religious club, but the moral shape of the world, well, then we can move from the back foot to the front foot. We need not be apologetic or defensive. Because we are not trying to impose our ideas upon anybody. We are simply saying to people, this is how the world is made, this is how human beings are; in lining up with this understanding of sex we will find blessing; in neglecting or rejecting it, we will find curse. As Jesus said of the Sabbath, so we can say of marriage, that marriage is made for men and women, not men and women for marriage.

So let us not be ashamed to be Bible Christians. The great Dutch Prime Minister Abraham Kuyper once famously said, 'There is not one square inch of the entire creation about which Jesus Christ does not cry out, "This is mine! This belongs to me!" '

We must hold on to the word of God, for only in this word fixed for ever in Creation, is security to be found. All other ground is sinking, shifting, and insecure. And so the singer does hold on; and the second half of the section majors on this holding on.

B. Because the world rests on the word, I may safely rest in the word forever (vv. 93-96).

Because the world rests on the word 'forever' (first word of v. 89), the believer who remembers and heeds these words 'forever' (first word of v. 93) is absolutely safe.

Leviticus 18:5 promises life to all who do the Covenant word of God. This promise was misunderstood by the legalists, such as Paul's opponents in Galatia. But in a profound sense, our singer can affirm that he *has* done the word (as Abraham in Gen. 26:5, and David in 1 Kings 3:14), and therefore by those precepts God *has* given him life as he promised to do. He is not claiming to have kept every commandment perfectly. But he is claiming that by the grace and mercy of God, he is faithful to the Covenant, and he has kept faith with the LORD. In other words, he is a believer and has responded as the Law always intended us to respond, by casting ourselves on the mercy of God believing his promises of the Christ to come.

Verse 94 puts Covenant faithfulness another way, very concisely: 'I am yours' (literally, 'I – to you'). He appeals on the basis of Covenant relationship, 'I am yours', between you and me there is an unbreakable bond. He has upon him God's own stamp and hallmark. And because he is tied to the LORD by Covenant, he prays, 'save me, for I have sought your precepts', that is, my direction of life is towards them; I study them, apply myself to them, seeking not only to understand them but to do them. I seek them because I seek him (cf. v. 2 'those who seek him'; cf. vv. 10, 45). This is a mark of a believer.

Verse 95 reminds us the enemies are still here. 'The wicked lie in wait to destroy me,' as they were in verse 61 when their cords ensnared him, and as they will be again in verse 110 when they lay a snare, and as they did with Daniel, and supremely with Jesus. But even as they lie in wait for him, he is not taken up with them and their threats; his concern is with the word of God: 'I consider your testimonies.' The enemies watch him; but he does not watch them. He understands the testimonies and he is attentive to them. The wicked attend to me with evil intent. But I do not repay their attentiveness with a reciprocal attentiveness to them. No, I attend to his testimonies.

There is here a double attentiveness, a double waiting. They wait for me, and I wait upon God. This asymmetrical attentiveness is perhaps the key to pastoral care; we want to turn the attention of our fellow believers away from their problems and towards their LORD. When under pressure, my instinct is to be preoccupied by the causes of the pressure, to become obsessed even with them, paranoid, more and more anxious. But the response is to consider the testimonies. The enemies look horizontally at me, as it were from behind the ambush hedge. But I look up to the LORD and his word. And therefore I am kept safe.

The reason it is worth attending to the LORD and his word is vividly expressed in verse 96, which is the climax of this great section: 'To all all-ness I see a cutting off, but wide your commandment exceedingly.' The word translated 'a cutting off', or a limit or end, is used in Exodus 12:41 of the 'end' of a period of time. The first half of the verse is clearly true in the experience of all people. To all all-ness, all perfection, every human project, there is a limit, a cutting off. Whether it be an end in time (because of death) or a limit in space (because of rival projects), every human project ends in failure. Even the empire of Alexander the Great, who is supposed to have wept because there were no more worlds to conquer, came to an end. Enoch Powell was right to say that every political biography is the story of failure in the end. The greatest sporting heroes in history lost in the end; always there was a final victory and then no more. One day Tiger Woods will no longer win. Even the most brilliant scientific theory does not last unmodified for ever. Every human project hits the buffers at last. Every philosophy fails in the end. All projects of Christian service end in failure, humanly speaking.

If we are wise, we will pray with Psalm 39:4, 'O LORD, make me to know my end' (the same word, 'my cutting off'); help me to grasp my mortality, my limits, what is the measure of my days. Derek Kidner comments that Psalm 119:96a could almost be a summary of the book of Ecclesiastes.

And yet, 'wide your commandment exceedingly'. That is, your commandment is broad without limit, limitless in time and space and profundity. Here alone in the universe is a perfection without end, an all-ness to which there is no cutting off. 'Of the increase of his government there will be no end' (the same word, no limit) (Isa. 9:7). The career of the Lord Jesus will not end in failure. And the word is the testimony to that. And therefore if I direct my ambitions and energies to his work, if my work is 'in the Lord', then finally it will not be 'in vain' (1 Cor. 15:58).

It is interesting to note that the word I have translated here 'wide' (v. 96) is linked to the words for 'enlarge my heart' in verse 32, and 'a wide place' in verse 45. And the reason the word of God opens up this broad vista, this wide place, an enlarged heart, is that it is the foundation of the universe. And it is the foundation of the new creation, in which the curse of death will be no more. It is as if God says, 'You can go anywhere you like, but you will never get outside the sphere where my commandment rules.' The logic is not dissimilar to the LORD's speeches in Job 38–41, exploring all the wild extremities of the Created Order, but never beyond the Creator's power and authority.

The doctrine of this section is wonderful news. I remember reading a sceptical book in which the author spoke scathingly of Christians, 'fiddling around in Bible land as the world burns'. But 'Bible land' is the Created Order land. The word of God gives the only reliable map to the world as it is. We need not fear the lie, 'It only works in church'.

And, as we shall see in the next section, the effect of this word on the human heart is wonderful.

PERSONAL RESPONSE QUESTIONS

1. Are you convinced that the word of God really works any-where and with anyone? In what areas do you find this most difficult? How does this section help?

2. What evidence have you seen in the world and in people you know, that the moral standards of God really work, bringing blessing when obeyed and curse when ignored?

13

Section 13:
Wisdom without Limit
(vv. 97-104)

Mem

[97]Oh how I love your *instruction*!
    All the day it is my meditation.
[98]More than my enemies I am wise by your *commandment*,
    for it is ever with me.
[99]More than all my teachers I have insight,
    for your *testimonies* are my meditation.
[100]More than the elders I have understanding,
    for I keep your *precepts*.

[101]I hold back my feet from every evil way,
    in order to keep your *word*.
[102]I do not turn aside from your *judgments*,
    for you have taught me.

[103]How sweet are your *promises* to my taste,
    sweeter than honey to my mouth!
[104]Through your *precepts* I get understanding;
    therefore I hate every false way.

Section 13 follows logically from Section 12. In Section 12 we rejoiced with the singer that the world rests upon the word, that the word rules the world, and not just our little ghetto. The word on which we rest our confidence rules the world in which we live. In verse 95 he says, 'I consider your testimonies'. He studies them and directs his attentive ear to hearing and heeding them. Now in this section we see the result: wisdom (v. 98), insight (v. 99), and understanding (vv. 100, 104), which are synonyms.

There is here a quiet reflective feel, with no urgent petition but just a peaceful resting in glorious truth.

As so often, I think this section divides in two. The first four verses speak of a greater wisdom; the second four of the practical outflow of that wisdom in life.

A. Delightful study of the word of God brings wisdom without limit (vv. 97-100).

The Hebrew letter *mem* is sometimes used before a word to introduce a comparison, such as 'more than'. In this section we see a threefold 'more than' in verses 98, 99, 100.

Verse 97, 'Oh how I love your instruction! All the day it is my meditation', the object of my musing, my study. He is a 'Bible moth Christian', devouring scripture as a moth left in the wardrobe without mothballs devours clothing (the term first applied to John Wesley's Holy Club). 'All the day' is emphatic: 'all the day it is my meditation'. All day long it is in my thoughts. And I love it. He says that twelve times in the psalm, eleven times of his word (vv. 47, 48, 113, 119, 127, 140, 159, 163, 165, 167), and once of his name (v. 132) – because love for him is love for his name and his name is known in his word. He loves God, and so he loves his word.

This love for God's word is a great proof of love for God. If a man says he loves God, but neglects his word, his love must be called into question. The world has many things to excite our love. Only the work of God in the heart of the believer will excite us with love for his word.

And a Bible moth Christian becomes a wise Christian. Again and again in this psalm the word of God is spoken of a something of great value. This reminds us of very similar language used in Proverbs (e.g. 2:1-15; 8:18) and Job 28 about the value of wisdom.

A Bible moth Christian becomes a wise Christian because it is by Wisdom that the world was made (Prov. 8:22-31). We see this in Psalm 104:24, 'O LORD, how manifold are your works! In wisdom have you made them all.' Sometimes in the Bible, Wisdom (which is synonymous with Understanding) is what we might call Wisdom with a capital 'W'. In the imagery of the Old Testament, this Wisdom means something like the Blueprint or Architecture of the Universe, as in Proverbs 3:19: 'The LORD by wisdom founded the earth; by understanding he established the heavens.' When God built the Universe, like a building, he did so according to the blueprint called Wisdom. Wisdom is the fundamental underlying Order according to which the Universe is constructed. This is deeper than just an Order in its material composition (which is the subject of the study of the material sciences); for this Order extends also to the moral and spiritual dimensions of existence. It is metaphysical as well as physical.

For the idea that this world might just have order in its material aspect (the subject of the physical sciences) but not in its moral and relational aspects would be unthinkable to the ancient (or modern) believer. Just as the physical scientist pursues the project of science in the belief that there is order to be discovered (which is why so much of the modern scientific enterprise has roots in Christian soil), so the believer lives on this earth in the conviction that it is finally not a chaotic universe, but one built upon an underlying and majestic order.

Sometimes we speak of the architecture of a piece of hardware or software. By this we mean the underlying structure, such that, if we understand it, we shall grasp why it behaves and responds as it does. When my laptop crashes, I have no idea what is going on. It might as well be inhabited by a legion of demons, for all I know. I become a practical animist, because

I have no understanding. But when someone who understands it comes to repair it, if they know the architecture (how the hardware and software are structured and work), then they can mend it. Wisdom is the shape of the universe.

In verses 98, 99, 100 we see a threefold reason why he loves it so much. Here are three parallel comparisons. First, verse 98, 'More than my enemies, I am wise, by your commandment, for it is ever with me.' We fear that our enemies know better than us how to make the best of a difficult world, that they will steal a march on us by being more street-wise, that our enemies have an edge on us because they are unconstrained by biblical morality; and yet in scripture we have the resource to make us wiser than them, to know in practice how to live in the world as it is. To be focused on the Bible is not to be taken out of engagement with this world with all its conflict; it is to be enabled for precisely this world.

The commandment that stands forever in the heavens (v. 89), is forever before me as I meditate on it. And the result is that I become wiser than my enemies. The word gives me access to the Architecture of the world. And therefore I need have no fear. If I want deeply to understand the world, I must love the word. If I want deeply to understand human beings, I must love the word. My enemies may be very clever. But God will turn their 'wisdom' into foolishness (1 Cor. 1:18–2:4). When David was threatened by the wisdom of one of the wisest counsellors around (Ahitophel) he prayed, 'O LORD, please turn the counsel of Ahitophel into foolishness.' (1 Sam. 15:31). And he did.

Second, verse 99, 'More than all my teachers I have insight, for your testimonies are my meditation', that is objects of study to me. This is the great undermining of hierarchy in the Christian church. There is a theology of the word here. If the source of my teacher's teaching is my teacher's wisdom, then I as his pupil will never get beyond him. But if God is my teacher, which is what happens when the Bible is taught, then I may well get beyond my human teacher. Calvin wisely noted that the fact that some Bible students grow in understanding beyond their Bible teachers is a kind of proof that God is the Teacher. When Jesus' family heard him they asked, 'Where did this man get this wisdom?' (Matt. 13:54). The answer is: he got it from the word of God, as any other believer does. He did not get his wisdom by some heavenly download; he got it from the Old Testament. We see an example of this when we hear him answer the tempter by the word of God (Matt. 4:1-11). He got his wisdom from the word of God. And we may do the same.

This wisdom is hidden from 'the wise and understanding', those who think they can get it without scripture; and it is revealed to 'little children', the nobodies who will come empty handed to scripture praying, 'Lord, teach me, teach me, teach me' (Matt. 11:25). This is why we are to call no man 'Rabbi', that is to defer to him as the authoritative source of guidance or wisdom, because we have one teacher (Matt. 23:8).

Commenting on 1 John 2:27 ('you have no need that anyone should teach you ...') Augustine wrote: 'There is here, my brothers, a great mystery on which to meditate: the sound of my voice strikes your ears, but the real Teacher is within. Do not think that anyone learns anything from another human being. We can draw your attention by the sound of our voice; but if within there is not the One who instructs, the noise of our words is in vain ... The internal Master who teaches is Christ the Teacher; his inspiration teaches. Where his inspiration and anointing are not found, the external words are in vain.'

Third, verse 100, 'More than the elders' (the ones in whom we might expect to find wisdom, the grey heads, AV 'the ancients'), 'I have understanding, for I *keep* your precepts.' Notice that understanding comes not just from hearing the word, but from *keeping* it, from hearing with doing (James 1:22-25). God gives understanding to those who will to obey. As Jesus said in John 7:17, 'If any man's will is to do God's will, he will know...'.

So in three ways in the first half he rejoices in the greater wisdom accessible by the word that made the world. There is no hierarchy of dependency in the Christian church, no monopoly of wisdom held by priests or scholars. Access to the word gives access to wisdom without limit. As William Tyndale famously said, 'A ploughboy with the Bible would know more of God than the most learned ecclesiastic who ignored it.'

The story is told of a vicar who was trying to help an elderly parishioner who had become a Christian late in life. So he gave him a Bible Commentary. He was a little worried how the old man would cope with the Commentary. So next time they met he asked him how he was getting on. 'Well,' said the elderly parishioner, 'it certainly is a hard book, a very hard book indeed. But I do find that the Bible sheds some light on it.'

This superior wisdom is found (v. 97) by meditating on the word. This is what Joshua was told to do: 'Do not let this book of the Law depart from your mouth; meditate on it day and night, so that you may be careful to do everything written in it. Then you will be prosperous and successful' (Josh. 1:8). This is what the singer does in Psalm 1, who delights in the law of the LORD and meditates on it day and night. He is like a tree planted by streams of water. This is what Timothy is told to do in 2 Timothy 2:7: 'Think over what I am saying, for the Lord will give you insight into all this.'

This word 'meditation' has been hijacked by non-Christian religions. It is important to be clear about the differences between Christian meditation and non-Christian, particularly the meditative techniques of Eastern religions. Here are two. First, Eastern meditation is a technique. There are exercises to be done, methods to be followed. Christian meditation is not a technique with rules, but a relationship with living dynamics. Second, Eastern meditation is fundamentally passive; one gives oneself up completely, lets go. We seek to disconnect, to empty ourselves. We put the mind into neutral.

But Christian meditation is active. We do not empty our minds; we fill them thoughtfully with God's truth. We do not lose our attention but focus and concentrate it. We do not seek relaxation but self-giving attentiveness to the word of God. We do not let ideas float around with no fixed direction. We fix them in the word, the works, the promises, the commandments, the self-revelation of God. Christian meditation is not an excursion without map or boundaries. It is a journey with a clear map and definite boundaries. James Packer defines it like this. 'Meditation is the activity of calling to mind, and thinking over, and dwelling on, and applying to oneself, the various things that one knows about the works and ways and purposes and promises of God. It is an activity of holy thought, consciously performed in the presence of God, under the eye of God, by the help of God, as a means of communion with God. Its purpose is to clear one's mental and spiritual vision of God, and to let His truth make its full and proper impact on one's mind and heart.'

John Bunyan in his writings was a man of one book. Although he wrote sixty books, he said, 'I have not for these things fished in other men's waters (that is, as we might say, I have not read all the secondary literature); my Bible and my Concordance are my only library in my writings.' Charles Spurgeon used to read *The Pilgrim's Progress* every year. He commented of Bunyan, 'He had studied our Authorised Version ... till his whole being was saturated with Scripture; and though his writings are charmingly full of poetry, yet he cannot give us his *Pilgrim's Progress* – that sweetest of all prose poems – without continually making us feel and say, 'Why, this man is a living Bible!' Prick him anywhere; and you will find that his blood is Bibline, the very essence of the Bible flows from him. He cannot speak without quoting a text, for his soul is full of the Word of God.' The singer was like that. And we may be too, if we develop habits of Bible reading and of mulling over the scriptures day by day and week by week.

So here is a great motivation to Bible study. When we immerse ourselves in this wonderful book, we find we have the LORD for our instructor, and therefore have access to a greater wisdom than is to be found anywhere else on this earth. But there is a challenge in the second half of the section.

B. BIBLE WISDOM IS FOUND NOT JUST BY BIBLE STUDY BUT BY BIBLE LIVING (VV. 101-104).

The focus in verses 97-101 has been on study, musing, meditation, activities of the eye and mind and pen. But when verse 100b mentions 'keeping' God's precepts, the focus shifts from the study to the world outside, from the quiet time to the day ahead, from the sermon to the workplace. True understanding (v. 100), wisdom (v. 98), and insight (v. 99), are matters that never stop with the mind. To keep his word means a moral outworking of wisdom.

This is why this second section is bracketed by very practical and moral references to restraining his feet from every path of wickedness (v. 101a) and hating every path of deception or falsehood (v. 104b). This reminds us of the old saying, 'This book will keep you from sin, or sin will keep you from this book'. The practical outflow of wisdom is not cleverness, but godliness. The one who is wise is not the one who knows a lot, but the one who lives like Christ.

Verse 101, 'I hold back my feet from every evil way, in order to keep your word.' The keeping of the word involves a very practical bodily holding back of the feet. To walk in the way is to keep my feet in the way (obviously).

Verse 102, 'I do not turn aside from your judgments, for you (emphatic) have taught me.' It is not I finally who hold back my feet, but you teaching me, you who work in me to will and to work your good pleasure, so that as you work in me I work out my salvation (Phil. 2:12, 13).

Verse 103, 'How sweet are your words to my taste, sweeter than honey to my mouth!' (cf. Prov. 24:13). This taste is, as Derek Kidner observes, an acquired rather than a natural taste. By nature we respond to the word of God as a child to mustard;

we spit it out. But as God works in us, and as we walk the way, so we acquire a taste for the word. And the more we taste, the more we want. His word is, as we say, 'moreish', so that we want to eat more and more. This is a challenge to us. By nature we find we love false ways. By grace we begin to hate them and to love the straight way.

It is important to think here why these words, which were what we would call Old Covenant words, were so utterly delightful to him. After all, in 2 Corinthians 3, Paul calls the Old Covenant the ministry of condemnation, the law that brings death. So how can he say here that it is like honey? The answer must be that this believer knew at least an anticipatory work of the Spirit on his heart, so that this word became not an outward letter, coming down in condemnation from Mt. Sinai, but a word of gospel that wrote the law upon his heart. And this word included within its scope the word of promise, the Covenant word that pointed forward to Christ. He rejoices in Christ as a believer in Christ looking with eager anticipation to the fulfilment of that promise in Christ.

And so he concludes in verse 104 by coming back to his main theme, 'Through your precepts I get understanding; therefore I hate every false way.' Notice how understanding affects not only our thoughts but also our affections. A right understanding of the word of God generates within us a cordial hatred of every false way.

This section builds on the doctrine of Section 12. Because the word underpins the world, an obedient lifelong study of the word makes available to the believer a wisdom without limit, a wisdom that issues in heartfelt godliness.

PERSONAL RESPONSE QUESTIONS

1. Does Bible study lead to Bible living for you?

2. Have you any experience of obedient Bible reading leading to a time of growing understanding, or of a period of disobedience leading to Bible blindness?

14

Section 14:
A Godly Determination
(vv. 105-112)

Nun

[105]A lamp to my feet is your *word*
and a light to my path.
[106]I have sworn an oath and confirmed it,
to keep your righteous *judgments*.

[107]I am deeply afflicted;
give me life, O LORD, according to your *word*!
[108]Accept my freewill offerings of praise, O LORD,
and teach me your *judgments*.

[109]I hold my life in my hand continually,
but I do not forget your *instruction*.
[110]The wicked have laid a snare for me,
but I do not stray from your *precepts*.

[111]Your *testimonies* are my heritage forever,
for they are the joy of my heart.
[112]I incline my heart to perform your *statutes*
forever, to the end.

A SURE WORD INSPIRES A GODLY DETERMINATION TO FOLLOW IT.

The theme of this section follows naturally from the last. We move now from stability (the theme of Section 12), through wisdom (the theme of Section 13) to a godly determination (the theme of this section). In Section 13 he rejoices in the greater wisdom of the word, a wisdom that leads to a changed life. Now he affirms forcefully his godly determination to walk in the way of that word. This tone of godly determination is seen in verse 105 (to walk by the light of the word), verse 106 (an oath sworn and confirmed to keep God's word), verse 109 ('I do not forget ...'), verse 110 ('I do not stray ...'), and above all climactically in verse 112 ('I incline my heart to perform your statutes forever, to the end.') This is the language of godly decision.

Verses 105 and 106 are in parallel, and verse 106 helps us understand the well-known verse 105: 'A lamp to my feet is your word and a light to my path.' The key point here is that this is about godliness more than it is about guidance. The words 'lamp' and 'light' seem to be associated not with guidance as a topic, but rather with Covenant safety in the context of danger. That is, the lamp and light are needed to keep the believer from straying off the path and into danger. So in Psalm 132:17 God promises 'a lamp for my anointed'. This means that his anointed King, his Christ, will grow in strength over his enemies (it is in parallel with a promise about his 'horn'). In Psalm 18:28 we read, 'it is you who light my lamp' in the context of salvation, victory, and refuge. The word 'path' here is used in Psalm 142:3, 'in the path where I walk they have hidden a trap for me'. So I need a lamp not to choose whether to go right or left, but so that I do not stumble as I keep going (morally) straight. I need a lamp because I am surrounded by a world that will otherwise make me stumble into danger. The same idea of being kept safe from danger by light is found in Psalm 56:13, 'For you have delivered my soul from death, yes, my feet from falling, that I may walk before God in the light of life.' And in Proverbs 6:23

we read that 'the commandment is a lamp and the teaching a light, and the reproofs of discipline are the way of life.'

We tend to use verse 105 as a text for talks on guidance. The problem is that for the most part the Bible does not directly help us with our guidance. We pretend it does, but actually it doesn't. It helps with simple decisions: should I murder my next door neighbour? The Bible answers that one! But most of the decisions in daily life the Bible does not directly make for us. And we should not pretend that it does. But what the Bible does do is to light our feet so that we do not stumble into doing wrong.

So this is not career guidance, but a lamp to keep me walking upright in the way, to protect me from the traps of darkness, and from falling into sin. When the devil tempted the Lord Jesus, it was the word of God that was a lamp to his feet and a light to his path. In verse 130 we see light in parallel with understanding as needed by the 'simple', those lacking wisdom. So this teaching about light links back to Section 13 with its theme of Wisdom.

It is only the word of God that can be this safe lamp for us. The counsels of our enemies will not (v. 98), for they are morally twisted and hostile. The counsels of our teachers and elders will not necessarily help (vv. 99, 100), for they may be human commandments made by men (cf. Mark 7:7; Isa. 29:13). Only the word of God can shed moral light on our path.

And therefore the proper response is verse 106, 'I have sworn an oath and confirmed it,'; that is, I have made a definite decision, a public decision, I have publicly pledged myself 'to keep your righteous judgments,' that is, to walk by the light of your lamp. This is the God-given grace-enabled purpose of my mind, that I will turn to this word as my lamp.

To make a pledge like this is not arrogant, if it is done by a believer in a spirit of faith, who prays with 2 Thessalonians 1:11 that our God may fulfil every resolve for good. We are not sufficient in ourselves to fulfil the vow we make. But it is good to make it and pray for God to enable us to keep it. We often do this in our hymns and songs. For example, we sing, 'Riches I heed not, nor man's empty praise' (in the hymn 'Be Thou My Vision'). This is not objectively true for those of us as we sing it. What we mean is that this is the desire of our hearts.

That this is not a cocky self-confidence is surely evident from verse 107, 'I am severely afflicted; give me life, O LORD, according to your word.' Again, we see the truth of verse 71 ('Good for me that I was afflicted'). He swears an oath, makes a good resolution; and then immediately is driven to cry for grace to keep it.

Verse 108 shows how dependence upon grace is accompanied by praise. 'Accept my freewill offerings of praise, O LORD, and teach me your judgments.' A freewill offering means one that does not need to be offered to pay for sin (e.g. Lev. 22:18; Exod. 35:29). It is an unforced, unconstrained, spontaneous outburst of gratitude and praise, the willing tribute of lips that love his name. So we have here a two-way dynamic of free praise and ongoing instruction.

Verse 109 echoes verse 107: 'I hold my life in my hand continually.' This idiom is the same as when we say, 'I take my life in my hands.' I take a big risk being a Christian, I risk my life. The same idiom is used by the witch of Endor when Saul secretly asks her to bring up Samuel from the dead (1 Sam. 8:21). No, she says, the king has forbidden this. If I do this, I 'take my life in my hands'. So for the singer here, to be a believer is to take a huge risk, as it is for many Christians across the world today. And I do it 'continually', he says. And as I do this, 'I do not forget your instruction.' Because your word is the only thread by which my fragile life is held fast to eternity.

The reason he takes his life in his hands in being a believer is spelt out again in verse 110: 'The wicked have laid a snare (a bird-trap, animal trap) for me, but I do not stray from your precepts.' Just north of Saigon (or Ho Chi Minh City) in Vietnam tourists can view some terrible man-traps put there in the Vietnam war to trap and maim American servicemen. They are horrible monuments to human cruelty. And they are a picture of what the world, the flesh and the devil will do to the believer if they can. It may be the snare of revenge which eats up and destroys a community (cf. Rom. 12:19-21). Or it may be the trap of unforgiveness, which destroys the unforgiving victim (cf. 2 Cor. 2:10f), or the stumbling block of lust (Matt. 7:27-30), or of pride (Matt. 18:1-6). In many ways the believer walks a path riddled with traps.

But in that path, the word of God is the lamp to light the way, that he may walk in it in safety. So that 'I do not stray from your precepts'. In verse 176 he uses the same verb 'stray' and says he *has* strayed like a lost sheep. So he is not claiming sinless perfection. But he is affirming in this section his strong determination to walk the way lit by the lamp of the word. As I walk this way, I will not finally stray.

In verse 111 he allows us to glimpse with him the end of the path. 'Your testimonies are my heritage forever, for they are the joy of my heart.' The word 'heritage' or 'inheritance' is used 59 times in the Old Testament and means a place or plot in the promised land. So in Exodus 32:13 Moses asks God to 'Remember Abraham, Isaac and Israel, to whom you swore ... all this land that I have promised I will give to your offspring, and they shall *inherit* it for ever.' So my 'heritage' is my place, my plot of land in the new creation.

What does he mean by saying 'your testimonies are my heritage'? He means that the written Covenant word is the Title Deed of the believer that guarantees to him his place in the new creation. Just as the Levites had no actual land, but the LORD was their inheritance, so the testimonies of the LORD are in anticipation and by way of guarantee, our heritage. And therefore they cause joy to well up in our hearts. This is why in verse 112 his affections are moved, his heart is inclined 'to perform your statutes, for ever, to the end' (or possibly 'as my reward'). The idea of a turning of the heart is important and appears here and in verses 36, 51, and 157. His heart is resolved for this because he understands the priceless value of this Title Deed to a place in the new heavens and new earth. And therefore it is a way to be walked with joy.

Personal Response Questions

1. Have there been times in your life when you have been aware of the Bible preventing you from falling into sin?

2. Does this section motivate you to make a fresh and definite determination to be wholehearted in your loving obedience to the Lord?

15

Section 15:
Loyalty and the Judgment
(vv. 113-120)

Samekh

113The divided I hate,
    but your *instruction* I love.
114You are my hiding place and my shield;
    I hope in your *word*.
115Depart from me, you evildoers,
    that I may keep the *commandments* of my God.

116Uphold me according to your *promise*, that I may live,
    and let me not be put to shame in my hope!
117Uphold me, that I may be safe
    and look intently at your *statutes* continually!

118You toss aside all who go astray from your *statutes*,
    for in vain is their cunning.
119Like dross you make to cease all the wicked of the earth,
    therefore I love your *testimonies*.
120My flesh shudders for terror of you,
    and I am terrified of your *judgments*.

In Section 14 the singer affirms his strong decision, the inclination of his heart, to walk the path lit by the lamp of the word. The theme of Section 15 is loyalty to the law. He lines himself up with God in his attitude to the ungodly who surround him.

The structure, unusually, would seem to be 3-2-3, with the middle couplet linked by the plea, 'Uphold me'.

A. LOYALTY TO GOD MEANS NO LOYALTY TO GOD'S ENEMIES (VV. 113-115).

The first three verses seem to go together in a sort of sandwich. On the outside there is reference to the ungodly, the double-minded or divided in verse 113, and the evildoers in verse 115. In between (v. 114) there is the loyal assertion that he can trust God. He hates, he is deeply averse to, those who have divided loyalties, fickle people, those like the people of Israel in Elijah's day who hobbled first on one leg, then on the other (1 Kings 18:21, Jerusalem Bible). Their double-mindedness is not an expression of honest uncertainty, but of a sinful heart (James 4:8). These people are like branches from a spreading tree. Their affections and loyalties reach out in different and contradictory directions. They are the opposite of the blessed man who seeks God with a whole heart (v. 2), with blameless-ness (v. 1).

To balance this aversion, he loves the instruction of the LORD (v. 114). It is a surprising contrast. After hating the double-minded we might expect him to love the single-minded. But the proper counterpart to hating God's enemies is to love God and his word. He does this, because, verse 114, 'You are my hiding place and my shield; I hope in your word.' The hiding place is the hidden secret place safe from strife and trouble (as often in the Psalms). It is the place where the singer shelters from 'the strife of tongues' (e.g. Ps. 31:20) or 'the day of trouble' (e.g. Ps. 27:5).

In a brief interlude from prayer, in verse 115 he cries out to his persecutors (whether or not they are listening), 'Depart from me, you evildoers, that I may keep the commandments of my God.' We have seen the cords of the wicked in verse 61, the pitfalls of the wicked in verse 85, and the snare of the wicked in verse 110. He says, 'I want to put distance between myself and the evildoers. That is to say, I will be in the world (I must be in the world), but I will not be of the world (John 15:19). And I will take great care about the kinds of partnerships and fellowships I join, so that I will not be unequally yoked with unbelievers (2 Cor. 6:14). He knows that 'friendship with the world is enmity with God' (James 4:4). He must keep this distance, 'that I may keep the commandments of my God'. He is aware of his weakness.

The distance he has in mind is more the avoidance of partnership than of physical proximity. He wants to avoid sharing their values and being infected by their fellowship. This cry points up an ongoing tension for believers who are in the world but must not let the world's values get into them. As D. L. Moody is supposed to have said, 'The ship is in the sea; but woe betide the ship if the sea gets into the ship.' The litmus test is the direction of our affections, as is seen in verse 113. So long as we experience an aversion to all who are not single-minded in loving God, and so long as we feel a warm love for his word, we are safe.

That is a challenge to us to choose the kinds of friendships we make, and the kinds of friendships that deepen. We want to make friendships with unbelievers, that they may be, as we say, bridges over which the Lord Jesus can cross. But those friendships will be different from the kind of fellowship we can have with believers, with those who fear his name.

B. LET HIM WHO THINKS HE STANDS TAKE HEED LEST HE FALL (VV. 116, 117).

Verse 116 and verse 117 are a parallel prayer to be upheld. It is a prayer not to be led into temptation but to be kept in the way of the LORD. Surrounded as he is by the double-minded, he knows the weakness of his own heart. He knows that by nature he too has a divided heart. Unless the LORD uphold him by his grace and according to his Covenant promise of perseverance, he cannot be safe. But the LORD has promised, and so both he and we may claim this promise when we echo this prayer. It is a prayer to be kept single-hearted, looking intently at his statutes continually, which is a way of speaking of whole-hearted attentiveness to the way and walk of the word of God. He knows that perseverance is only by grace given in answer to prayer.

C. WE SHOULD SHRINK IN FEAR FROM THE JUDGMENT ON THE WICKED (VV. 118-120).

Verse 118a and verse 119a are closely parallel. Here he takes a good look at the double-minded of verse 113, the evildoers of verse 115; but he looks at them now from God's point of view. He has said that he wants to keep distance from these people. And the reason is that they are in terrible danger.

Verse 118: 'You toss aside all who go astray from your statutes, for in vain is their cunning.' The world thinks such people are men and women of substance, really 'somebodies'. But in the sight of God they are tossed aside as nobodies, as the LORD did with the mighty men of Jerusalem at the time of exile (see Lam. 1:15, using the same word: 'The LORD rejected (tossed aside) all the mighty men in my midst'). The moment I go astray from his statutes, I leave the path and wander away, is the moment not only when I have tossed God aside; it is also, much more terribly, the moment when he tosses me aside. He gives me up to my choice (cf. Rom. 1:24, 26, 28). Their 'cunning' uses a word also used in Jeremiah (e.g. 8:5; 14:14; 23:26) of the false prophets. This may possibly be a hint that these enemies come from within the people of God, an enmity that is especially troubling and painful to the godly. In God's sight their cunning, their hostility, their attempts to trip him up, are in vain, because God will toss them aside.

Loyalty and the Judgment (vv. 113-120)

If verse 118 speaks of rejection, verse 119 speaks of value: 'Like dross you make to cease all the wicked of the earth, therefore I love your testimonies.' They think they are valuable like silver; but God counts them as dross. These wicked seem to themselves so important. They seem to the world so important and lasting, but you discard them like the dross they are, as you purify your people (cf. Isa. 1:22, 25; Ezek. 22:18f). You 'make them to cease', a word used in Psalm 8:2, 'you ... *still* the enemy and the avenger'; that is, you tell them to shut up, you silence them; and it is used of the rebuke to the arrogant enemies in Psalm 46:10, 'Be *still*, and know that I am God' (which does not mean a delightful quiet, as in some mystical meditation; it means, 'Shut up!') These wicked cause me so much trouble. They seem so weighty, so at the centre of things. And yet one day you will cause them to cease. You will tell them to shut up, as Jesus did to the storm.

Because God will do this, in verse 119b the singer speaks again of loving the judgments of God. That is, he loves the God who will act in justice to reject the wicked arrogant ones who ruin his world and oppress his people.

All this he knows. But as he meditates on this (cf. Ps. 3:17ff), his whole body trembles with dread and terror of the God who will do this. Verse 120 is an extraordinary verse: 'My flesh shudders for terror of you, and I am terrified of your judgments.' The only other Old Testament use of the word translated 'shudders' is in Job 4:15 where Eliphaz speaks of a spirit gliding past his face and the hair of his flesh standing up. It is the imagery of a horror movie. When he thinks of the judgment coming upon the double-minded, he shudders physically. He says, 'Dread of you makes my flesh creep, my skin shivers in fear of you, my hair stands on end for terror of you.' This terror is much stronger than the usual healthy reverent fear of the LORD. The word 'terror' is not 'the fear of the LORD', the reverent worshipful loving fear of the believer, the fear that is the beginning of wisdom. It is sheer dread, the terror that came upon Pharaoh's army in Exodus 15:16, the terror of the LORD of which Isaiah speaks in Isaiah 2:10, the terror of the wicked in Psalm 14:5. It is a very strong word. It is a strong terror. It is as if he looks over the edge of the Abyss, as we might gaze down a deep well-shaft or over a colossal cliff, and shrinks back in vertiginous trembling.

This terror follows the recollection in verses 118, 119 of the judgment of God on the ungodly. Even in the security of his walk with the LORD the very thought of this judgment is enough to make him tremble.

Calvin comments that, 'It is evidence of no common wisdom to tremble before God when he executes his judgments, of which the majority of mankind take no notice.'

In a very personal writing about confession, the nineteenth-century Scottish preacher Robert Murray McCheyne wrote, 'The falls of professors (i.e. professing Christians) into sin make me tremble. I have been driven away from prayer, and burdened in a fearful manner by hearing or seeing their sin. This is wrong. It is right to tremble, and to make every sin of every professor a lesson of my own helplessness, but it should lead me the more to Christ ...' I wonder if some felt that when Roy Clements left his wife, family, and pastorate. We ought to have done. For the judgment of God is a terrible thing. 'And how shall we escape if we neglect, if we fall away from, such a great salvation?' (Heb. 2:3).

This singer has understood that he should fear not the powerful human beings who can kill the body, but rather the one who has the power to destroy body and soul in hell (Luke 12:5). This is why he wants so desperately to keep his distance from the double-minded. As in Korah's rebellion (Num. 16), you have to choose. Either you distance yourself from him, or the earth opens up and you are destroyed (cf. 2 Tim. 2:19). Wholehearted devotion to the LORD is not an optional extra in the life of faith.

Do we feel this healthy terror? Or are we lulled into a cosy cooperation with the world, into a sense that we must not be

Loyalty and the Judgment (vv. 113-120)

too different, that we must learn to fit in, that it isn't helpful to our evangelism if our values are too different? Do we feel that it is better to be 'one of the boys (or girls)' and therefore accepted by the in-crowd? We ought to fix firmly in our hearts the terror the singer feels, the conviction that God tosses aside all who go astray. We do well to shudder for fear of him. For the one who is our hiding place and our shield (v. 114) will also be our terror if we stray. So we must cast ourselves on his grace daily to be kept in the way.

Personal Response Questions

1. In what practical ways do you need to keep distance from those who do not share God's values and love his word?

2. Can you echo the terror of verse 120 when you think of God's judgment on the wicked? How does this section help you to feel this more strongly and to respond appropriately?

16

Section 16:
The Longings of Loyalty
(vv. 121-128)

Ayin

¹²¹I have done *judgment* and righteousness;
  do not leave me to my oppressors.
¹²²Give a pledge to your servant of good;
  let not the insolent oppress me.
¹²³My eyes long for your salvation
  and for your righteous *promise*.
¹²⁴Deal with your servant according to your steadfast love,
  and teach me your *statutes*.

¹²⁵I am your servant; give me understanding,
  that I may know your *testimonies*!
¹²⁶It is time for the LORD to act,
  for your *instruction* has been broken.

¹²⁷Therefore I love your *commandments*
  above gold, above fine gold.
¹²⁸Therefore I consider all your *precepts* to be right;
  I hate every false way.

The theme of loyalty continues here. Notice how three times he describes himself as 'your servant' (vv. 122, 124, 125), the title of Covenant loyalty. The logic of saying 'your servant' is

(a) I know you are loyal to me, and therefore (b) I am loyal to you. I line myself up with your honour and I rest my destiny on your promises. So loyalty is a big theme here. And it is loyalty under terrible pressure.

The section divides naturally in two.

A. We know God will be loyal to us, and therefore long for the final rescue (vv. 121-124).

Each of these four verses expresses the same fundamental longing (v. 121, 'Do not leave me ...'; v. 122 ,'Give a pledge ...'; v. 123, 'My eyes long ...'; v. 124, 'Deal ... according to your steadfast love'). It is longing for rescue from oppression (v. 121, 'my oppressors'; v. 122, '... oppress me').

When he says in verse 121, 'I have done judgment and righteousness', this is not a claim to merit, but an evidence of grace. Fundamentally, he says, the direction of my life is characterized by 'judgment' (that is, keeping my decisions in line with God's published decisions in the law), and by 'right-eousness' (that is, treating other people aright). The fact that my life is actually like this is evidence of grace, for it would not be possible from my own moral resources. And because it is evidence of grace, he prays, 'do not leave me to my oppressors'. This is, if you like, the testimony of a good conscience (cf. Acts 23:1; 24:16). As John would put it, this believer is 'walking in the light' (1 John 1:7).

The prayer continues in verse 122: 'Give a pledge to your servant of good; let not the insolent oppress me.' None of the eight 'word of God' words occurs in this verse. The word 'pledge' takes their place. To give a pledge means to take responsibility for someone else, perhaps for their debt, to 'stand surety', to give a guarantee for my well-being; just as if I am in huge debt and you graciously 'stand surety' for me, it means you will guarantee the payment of my debt, if necessary by paying it yourself. So in Genesis 43:9 Judah says to Jacob about Benjamin, 'I will be a pledge of his safety.' In Proverbs 11:15 we read, 'Whoever puts up security (a pledge) for a stranger will surely suffer harm'; it is a costly thing to do. In Isaiah 38:14, when King Hezekiah is sick he prays, 'O LORD, I am oppressed; be my pledge of safety.' This is what Job asks for in Job 17:3, 'Lay down a pledge for me ... who is there who will put up security for me?' So Calvin paraphrases the prayer, 'Lord ... since the proud cruelly rush upon me to destroy me, interpose thyself between us, as if thou wert my surety.'

He is praying for the Cross. This prayer points forward to the day hundreds of years later when God did just that, in the person of his Son; when he took responsibility for our debts, and nailed them to the Cross. And because he did that, we know that our oppressors will not finally succeed. So to pray, 'Give your servant a pledge of good' is a prayer for the Cross of Christ. As Charles Spurgeon put it, 'We should have been crushed beneath our proud adversary the devil if our Lord Jesus had not stood between us and the accuser.' (There is a similar prayer in verse 154, 'plead my cause and redeem me'.)

Only when this pledge is given can he, or we, be kept safe from oppressors (v. 121b), no longer oppressed by the insolent (v. 122b). He longs for this pledge with all his being.

Verse 123: 'My eyes long for your salvation and for (the fulfilment of) your righteous promise' ('the fulfilment of' needs to be understood here). His eyes long (literally 'are full', brimming over with tears of longing, growing weak with the pain), as in verse 82 ('My eyes long for your promise; I ask, "when will you comfort me?" ') How vividly the eye expresses the emotions of the soul (cf. Deut. 34:7). But this man's eye is weak, dim, and full of tears as he longs for God's rescue.

And yet the rescue he longs for is not some haphazard maybe on, maybe off thing, something that a whimsical deity might do if he gets out of bed the right side in the morning. No, verse 123, is the fulfilment of his 'righteous promise'. This is not the desperate hoping against hope cry of the unbeliever. It is the confident prayer of the Christian, who can pray for rescue on the basis of rescue promised in the word of God. This is why in verse 124 he longs for 'steadfast love', that is the fulfilment of Covenant promise. In this context verse 124b, 'teach me your statutes' means much more than an intellectual learning, and includes the kind of teaching that leads me in the way of your statutes. When he instructs us and leads us in the way, it is an expression of his Covenant steadfast love.

This longing is not an optional extra for his spiritual life; it is the mainspring of his prayer. This is Christian spirituality, directed like a passionate arrow to the future. He wept, he watched, he waited, he looked to God alone, he looked eagerly, he looked long. And because the word of God assured him his looking would not be in vain, he never stopped longing.

B. Loyalty to God expresses itself in love for the Law (vv. 125-128).

The second half of this section perfectly balances the first. He knows the LORD is loyal to him, because the Covenant word of scripture tells him so. On that basis he longs for the promised rescue when the LORD himself will stand between this believer and his foes, on the Cross. And in the second half we learn more deeply just how and why he longs as he does.

Verse 125, 'I am your servant' – and that's why I can pray – 'give me understanding, that I may know your testimonies', that is, know them in experience, in walking their way, know not as a spectator but as a participant. To be given understanding is to be changed inside.

Verse 126, 'It is time for the LORD to act' (or, vocative: 'it is time for you to act, O LORD'). This is audacious! 'Lord God, Creator of the universe, it is time for you to get off your backside and do the job of judging the earth.' What a nerve! But it is the cry of the saints, 'your kingdom come!', 'Come, Lord Jesus!' That's what it means. 'It is time for the LORD to act.'

The Longings of Loyalty (vv. 121-128)

Is it not extraordinary that he allows us to pray like that? We might expect him to answer, 'Shut up! I will do it in my good time.' But actually he longs for us to pray like this. We ought to pray like this.

Notice the motivation of this prayer, which is not personal hurt. Why does he watch, wait, weep, and call on the LORD to act? Well, we say, because he's having a bad time. We would have written, 'because I am having a rotten time and it's very unfair.' But, as Calvin put it, 'our zeal is ... disordered whenever its moving principle is a sense of our own personal injuries.'

The reason he gives is deeper. It is focused not on his need, but on the LORD's glory: '...for your instruction has been broken'. Our concern is to be his honour above our comfort. We pray for judgment because we long for his honour. As a loyal lover of the LORD he is outraged at this insult to the dignity and majesty of God. He looks at the world and he sees how 'sin becomes fashionable, and a holy walk is regarded as contemptible puritanism; vice is styled pleasure' (Calvin). And he is filled with a holy anger and jealousy for the honour of God.

And then in verses 127, 128 we see what Derek Kidner calls, 'the logic of loyalty'. He is surrounded by people who despise God's law; and his response is to love that law all the more. The more the pressure grows to abandon it, the more passionately and delightedly he embraces it. He is deeply loyal. Verse 127, 'Therefore I love your commandments, above gold, above fine gold.' We saw that in verse 72 ('the law of your mouth is better to me than thousands of gold and silver pieces'). Now it is intensified: fine gold, the gold of Ophir (Isa. 13:12). As in Psalm 19:10, the words of God are, 'More to be desired ... than gold, even much fine gold.'

This value language is used of the Wisdom that is sought in Job 28:17 and offered in Proverbs 8:19. It is the value the Divine Lover has for his Beloved in Song 5:11, 15. If he values us like fine gold, ought we not to value his word the same?

In all this he is learning to appreciate the beauty of sheer rightness in the law of God. Verse 128, 'Therefore I consider all your precepts to be right; I hate every false way.' The only other use of this word 'right' in the Psalms is Psalm 5:8 'Lead me, LORD, in your righteousness because of my enemies; make your way *straight* (right) before me.' The right precept is like a signpost down a straight road, a morally upright road, a true road. It is the opposite of a twisted, deceitful way, the false way. And so Section 16 ends as Section 15 began, in verse 113, with a hatred of every false way, a hatred of those whose loyalties are divided.

As his hope is fixed on the future rescue of God, his affections are lined up with that future judgment. Because he longs for salvation then, he loves the commandments now. Because he expects judgment then, he hates every false way now. This is the dynamic that links his future expectation to his present behaviour.

We need to understand what the Reformers called 'the third use of the Law'.

In what they called the first use, the Law brings conviction of sin, brings us to our knees, shows us the holiness of God and our deep need for a Saviour. Important too is what they called the second use, the Law as the proper basis for the laws in our societies, showing us the moral grid. But this psalm is full of the third use of the Law, as a clear and delightful guide to the believer to show him or her how to live and please God.

So let's put these two halves of the section together. The theme is the longings of loyalty. He is God's servant, bound to the LORD by cords of loyal love which extend both from the LORD to him and from him to the LORD. Because they begin with the LORD's promised loyalty to him, he longs for the Cross. And because he is filled with answering jealous loyalty to the LORD, he is outraged at the unbelieving world around him and clings more devotedly than ever to this Covenant word.

The Longings of Loyalty (vv. 121-128)

The question for us is whether our spirituality, the way we relate to God, is shaped by the longings of loyalty. The test will be our grief at wickedness and our prayers for the judgment. What causes us grief? And what moves us to prayer? Is it frustrations at work, the inability to achieve what we want? Is it disappointments in relationships, which do not yield for us the fulfilment for which we had hoped? Or is it the breaking of God's law in our own lives and the lives of those around us? Is this what moves us to tears and makes prayer well up within us? This is biblical spirituality.

We ought to be deeply challenged by this mark of the believer soaked in the word of God. For the word of God stirs up in us and brings to the front of our affections the longings of loyalty. Do we in our church fellowships long passionately for God? Do we as individual Christians long urgently and desperately for God? Because if we do we will pray.

Jesus taught this in Luke 18:1-8 using the image of the widow in an unfair world, desperate for justice, pestering the unjust judge until he gives way. 'How much more', says Jesus, 'ought the believer to pray to the judge of all the earth and not give up! When the son of man comes will he find faith on earth?' If the Lord Jesus were to return tomorrow, would he find in us that deep longing for God that pours itself out in prayer? Would he find our church meetings for prayer overflowing – overflowing with people so that we could not fit into our buildings, and overflowing with prayer? Or would he find a bunch of lukewarm orthodox respectables going through the motions? The test of our faith is our prayer meetings. The singer would have been there every time.

PERSONAL RESPONSE QUESTIONS

1. Are you fiercely loyal to the LORD? How does (or would) this show itself in your prayers?

2. How closely linked are your love for the LORD and your love for his word?

17

Section 17:
Grace and Loyal Grief
(vv. 129-136)

Pe

¹²⁹Your *testimonies* are wonderful;
    therefore my soul keeps them.
¹³⁰The unfolding of your *words* gives light;
    it imparts understanding to the simple.

¹³¹I open my mouth and pant,
    because I long for your *commandments*.
¹³²Turn to me and be gracious to me,
    as is your *judgment* with those who love your name.

¹³³Keep steady my steps according to your *promise*,
    and let no iniquity get dominion over me.
¹³⁴Redeem me from man's oppression,
    that I may keep your *precepts*.

¹³⁵Make your face shine upon your servant,
    and teach me your *statutes*.
¹³⁶My eyes shed streams of tears,
    because people do not keep your *instruction*.

This section begins with wonder and ends in tears. Mostly it is wonder; the tears come only in the last verse. The theme of wonder at grace appears with the 'light' of verse 130, the plea to 'be gracious' in verse 132, and the shining face of God in verse 135, which hold together the light of God's word and the light of God's face.

A. We are to pray for the word to give light (vv. 129-132).

The first half is a prayer for the gracious gift of the word poured into the heart to change the life. Verse 129, 'Your testimonies are wonderful'; they are wonderful in their origin, breathed out by the living God; they are wonderful in their nature, as utterly reliable; and they are wonderful in their effects, bringing light into dark lives. They are full of the 'wonders' of God's rescue (cf. v. 18). And 'therefore (that is why) my soul keeps them'; that is why I want to go this way.

And they do their wonderful work of rescue by shining light into dark lives and changing hard hearts. Verse 130: 'The unfolding of your words gives light; it imparts understanding to the simple.' Have you sat in a very dark room? And outside, out of the window or in the corridor, there is a very bright light. And someone just begins to open the door or curtain and the light floods in. Even a crack in the curtain or door and the light floods in, it is so bright. The word of God is like that. You don't have to wait until you are an expert before you begin to get understanding from the word of God. Anyone who is 'simple', which means here someone who knows their need, who has no conceit, no self-confidence, no arrogant certainty that they already know how to run the world, will benefit even from the first entrance of the word of God.

I am 'simple'. By nature I am a fool. I am spiritually obtuse. And it is only by the word of God that I, a fool, will become wise and gain understanding; I who by nature walk in darkness will be given light, as his word is 'unfolded', opened up to me. It is not shouted to me from outside, but fed to me by his Spirit into my heart. The word for 'entrance' or 'unfolding' may well have the sense of the word being expounded. What an incentive this is to us to read our Bibles and to go where the word is unfolded and expounded for us!

We learn from this verse, first, that when the word enters the chambers of the human spirit and heart, light floods in. But we also learn that there needs to be an unfolding and an entrance. It is not enough that the words be read and heard; they must be allowed an entrance. As we learn in the parable of the sower, it is possible to hear but not understand (Matt. 13:19); and indeed it is possible also to hear and receive with joy, and yet the word takes no root (Matt. 13:20, 21). The word may be blocked by pride, by laziness, by a sense that I am not so 'simple', not so much in need. But whenever we come to the word on our knees, knowing our simplicity and foolishness, and pray, 'Lord, teach me, teach me, teach me,' then the LORD gives his word an entrance; and then there is light.

This entrance demands a double work of the Spirit of God. On the one hand, the word needs to be opened up to us; and therefore we need to pray for preachers and teachers. On the other, we need to open ourselves up to it; and so we need to pray for hearers. Only when God works in both preachers and hearers does this wonderful double 'unfolding' take place and light flood in.

And therefore (v. 131), 'I open my mouth and pant because I long for your commandments.' Like our hungry dog as meal time approaches, he looks longingly to be fed from the word. He really understands that it is only in the word of God that he will be enlightened, that he will move from being a fool to being a wise man, that he will find understanding to live in the real world as he ought to live. He longs not only for these words just as words, but as words that are 'unfolded', opened up to his understanding and therefore to his life as well. He longs and pants not just for an intellectual grasp of the words of God, but for these words to be unfolded into his life and walk, to change him.

Because he knows that the unfolding of the word of God is a work of grace he now prays, verse 132, 'Turn to me and be gracious to me'; in the context here this turning of God to him is expressed in the grace of Bible understanding. I do not deserve to understand my Bible and for it to take root in my life; but I may pray for it as a gift of grace as God turns to me.

He prays for this grace, '... as is your judgment with those who love your name.' This is a significant use of *mishpat* (judgment, decision), which reveals something important about how the singer understood the word of God. The word or judgment of God means here God's decision as judge. And the written word of God reveals to us the settled decision of God as judge, that he will always turn in grace and favour to the one who loves his name. So when he prays for this turning, it is not a random or whimsical prayer, but a prayer precisely in line with the revealed words and ways of God.

That is, he may not feel the LORD's presence; he may not experience his presence in wonderful circumstances or mystical ecstasy. If he is guided by his feelings and experience he will often conclude that God does not love him. But he knows from the word of God, the judgment of God, the character of God, that the way God consistently responds to those who love his name is with grace. That is why he can pray as he does.

Isn't that lovely? With those who love his name, his revealed name, given in his word, that is, who love him, it is his way, his judgment, his sovereign decision, to turn and be gracious. First, he turns us to him with the gift of repentance. And then he turns to us and smiles his grace. And he shows that grace by pouring his life-changing word into our open panting mouths. How we need that!

In the second half of the section the camera moves back to show not just the believer and his God, but also the forces that threaten that relationship.

B. WE NEED LIGHT BECAUSE WE ARE SURROUNDED BY DARKNESS (vv. 135-138).

Verse 133, 'Keep steady my steps' – as I walk the way – 'according to your promise', your Covenant promise to keep me steady, 'and let no iniquity get dominion over me.' Like Cain, sin is crouching at the door and desires to master me (Gen. 4:6). Only by the grace of God will my steps stay steady and iniquity will not get dominion over me. We are surrounded without, and filled within, with passions that threaten to engulf us. Whether these passions be covetousness, lust, pride, or whatever, we too need to pray, 'Keep steady my steps.' Perhaps as we walk past a bookstall knowing that it contains literature that will just stir up lust, we can pray, 'Lord, keep steady my steps.' As we make lifestyle decisions about getting or spending money, 'Lord, keep steady my steps.'

In praying 'and let no iniquity get dominion over me', he is praying to walk joyfully under grace rather than law. Why does iniquity gain dominion over me? The answer is in Romans 6. Sin is a slave-master. And the power, the Weapon of Mass Destruction of sin, is death. But in the gospel death is destroyed, and him who has the power of death, that is the devil (Heb. 2:14). Sin will have no more dominion over me, because I am not under law but under grace (Rom. 6:14). In some anticipatory fashion it seems that this believer prays this gospel truth.

The slavery of sin and the oppression of his human enemies seem to be closely linked, as we see from the parallel verse 134: 'Redeem me' – pay the price, give the pledge (v. 122) – 'from man's oppression' (literally, the oppression of Adam, the oppression that comes both outside from hostile people and inside from being in Adam's sinful line), 'that I may keep your precepts'. Because, unless he redeems me, if it were not for his grace, I could not keep his precepts. This is the walk of dependence upon grace from first to last.

To walk with steady steps free from the dominion of sin, is blessing. This is why in verse 135 he echoes the blessing of Aaron from Numbers 6:22-27: 'Make your face shine upon your servant, and teach me your statutes.' The grace of God means a shining in the face of God as he looks upon his servant. It is very personal, because there is no such thing as 'grace' in the abstract; there is only the personal gracious God. As he shines on us by his grace, he teaches us his statutes. It is a work of grace when God shapes our lives to walk the way of his word.

This work of grace happens in a fallen world. As the singer basks in the light of the word and the light of the LORD, he weeps for the darkness. Verse 136, 'My eyes shed streams of tears,' (canals of tears) 'because people do not keep your instruction.' This grief is the flip side of passionate love and wonder at the grace of the word of God. This last verse is powerful and surprising. We see a shift of focus, from upwards to a loving God, to outwards to disobedient people. The more the singer is aware of the great personal blessing of God's face shining on him, God turning to him, God keeping his steps steady, the more desperately sad he is to contemplate those around him who do not go this way.

He weeps and weeps and weeps, literally 'channels' or 'canals' of tears flowing from his eyes. He weeps not because he is in pain, not because those around don't happen to share his religious hobby, but because they do not keep God's instruction. As Lot grieved over Sodom and his righteous soul was tormented (2 Pet. 2:8), and as the Lord Jesus wept over Jerusalem (Luke 19:41-44), so his eyes shed streams of tears at a lost world around who could not care less about God's law.

I wonder if we do this. Perhaps the nearest many of us get to this is when someone close to us goes astray from God's way. Perhaps a beloved son or daughter, or a close friend who turns from, or cares nothing for, God's law. Perhaps then our eyes actually fill with tears. It is no bad thing when they do.

Calvin wisely reminds us that we should 'let our grief begin at ourselves', as we weep at the darkness within our own hearts. If we weep only for others, it may lead to smugness or self-righteousness. So we must weep first for sin within ourselves. I remember hearing of a fellow-minister whose wife would sometimes go into his study while he was praying and preparing, and would find him on his knees weeping for his sin and for the sin of others. Spurgeon comments, 'That man is a ripe believer who sorrows because of the sins of others.'

We need this godly grief! How little and how weakly I share it. How attractive is wickedness to me, and how little I grieve. How little am I stirred as Paul was in Athens (Acts 17:16) because the city was full of idols, because the instruction of the LORD was not kept. Does it move me to tears? It ought to. And as the singer longs to be kept in the way of the word, he grieves deeply over a world that does not share that longing.

PERSONAL RESPONSE QUESTIONS

1. What experience do you have of the Bible shining light into your life?

2. To what extent do you have a panting hunger for the word of God, and a tear-filled grief because others don't keep it?

18

Section 18:
The Loyal Love of Goodness
(vv. 137-144)

Tsadhe

[137]Righteous are you, O Lord,
   and your *judgments* are straight.
[138]You have commanded your *testimonies* in righteousness
   and in deep faithfulness.

[139]My zeal consumes me,
   because my foes forget your *words*.
[140]Your *promise* is deeply well tried,
   and your servant loves it.

[141]I am small and despised,
   yet I do not forget your *precepts*.
[142]Your righteousness is righteous forever,
   and your *instruction* is true.

[143]Trouble and anguish have found me out,
   but your *commandments* are my delight.
[144]Righteous are your *testimonies* forever;
   give me understanding that I may live.

WE MAY TRUST THE SURE WORD OF GOD

This section celebrates the sheer goodness, rightness and straightness of the word of God. The theme is suggested by the letter *tsadhe*, which begins the word group 'righteousness' or 'righteous'. The first verse (v. 137) and the last verse (v. 144) begin with the word 'righteous'. It appears also in verse 138 ('You have commanded your testimonies in righteousness'), and twice in verse 142 ('Your righteousness is righteous forever'). A very similar idea is taught in the word translated 'straight' in verse 137, the word 'faithfulness' in verse 138, the word 'well tried' in verse 140 and the word 'true' in verse 142.

God cares passionately about justice. 'A just weight is his delight' (Prov. 11:1). We too ought to share this delight, and also his hatred of injustice. We ought to care about these things more than we do. I read a prayer letter recently from a young unmarried woman missionary in a corrupt communist country. She lives on her own in a country village. Recently her home was burgled and important items stolen. She now knows two things. First, that the thieves are local drug dealers, who have the items in their house nearby. But second, that she has no prospect of justice, because these men are related to government ministers and are untouchable by the law. We ought to be hotly indignant that justice will not be done.

So what does it mean to affirm that the word of God is righteous? It means first, that what it says is cognitively true not false. But much more deeply than that, the righteousness of God means his gracious activity to rescue those who trust in him. Righteousness is not only an attribute of God's character; it is also an activity of his person. It is not some abstract Olympian quality, but what he does, the right judgments he makes in governing the world. You cannot be righteous in scripture without doing righteousness. The righteousness of God means something like his trustworthiness in acting on behalf of those who call on him. We are to believe in the reliability of scripture, that we can rely on it; we can rest our present and our future on it, without fear of being let down. The righteousness of God means his utter dependability for all who are in right relation with him by faith in Christ.

All through the Old Testament one of the great puzzles was how God could act in righteousness to rescue unrighteous people. It is the puzzle the gospel answers and Paul expounds from Romans 1:16 through to Romans 3:26. This puzzle was only answered at the Cross, which revealed the righteousness of God and how he could at the same time be righteous and also count as righteous those who have faith in Jesus (Rom. 3:26). But even if he doesn't yet understand the logic of the Cross, our singer knows that the righteousness of God is true. What the singer delights in and sings is the righteousness of Christ prefigured in the Old Covenant word.

Notice the effect this has on the singer in his struggles. Verse 137, 'Righteous are you, O LORD, your judgments are straight.' Because you yourself are the righteous God, we may be sure that your judicial decisions, your decisions about how you run the world, will be made uprightly. They will be straight not crooked. For, verse 138, 'You have commanded (the same verb from which we get 'commandments') your testimonies in righteousness, and in deep faithfulness' (that is, exceeding faithfulness, as faithful as faithful can be). The whole thing is straight. There is no leaning tower of Pisa here, no twistedness, no possibility of being let down or misled, nothing out of true. The word of God is reliable because God is reliable.

Our response to this is not complacency but zeal. Verse 139 'My zeal consumes me', I share in my spirit something of the righteous jealousy of God. I yearn hotly for the honour of the name of God. Paul felt this 'divine jealousy' when he pleaded for the purity of the church in Corinth (2 Cor. 11:2). This zeal arises 'because my foes forget your words.' This does not mean 'forget' in a purely cerebral sense, for they may even quote scripture as the devil did to Jesus (Matt. 4:6). It means 'forget' in the biblical sense of not heeding them, not obeying them, not walking by them. And so, like Phinehas in Numbers 25, he is consumed with a right zeal or jealousy for God. He is full of righteous indignation that this upright word of this righteous God should be despised.

Verse 140, 'Your promise is well tried, and your servant loves it.' The word of God is 'well tried', tried and tested, tested and true. You can rest on this and it won't collapse under you. You can build your life in obedience to this promise and when the storms of judgment come it will not collapse, like a house built on sand (Matt. 7:24-27) or like a wall that is bulging and on the point of collapse (Isa. 30:13). We can rejoice in the well-tried character, the security of the justice of God.

When I visited Japan in 2006, there was a well-publicised court case going on. A prominent architect was arrested and accused of falsifying the earthquake-proofing certificates of a number of high-rise buildings in the Tokyo area. Japan is very prone to earthquakes, and it is only the high quality building standards that protect the population from injury or death. But this man had falsified the certificates, so that buildings that claimed to be earthquake-proof were nothing of the sort.

That is a picture of idolatry. An idol, like a high-rise building, says to us, 'Come in here. Devote your life to my service. And in this fine impressive building you will be safe when the storms of life come.' The truth is that the first shake of the earth and the whole thing will fall down. But the Covenant of God is secure in Jesus Christ. In Christ we may live 'in Zion,' in the city that will be the richest place on earth when the earth is shaken (Hag. 2:6-9), where the only lasting kingdom will be established (Hag. 2:22, 23), the city that cannot be shaken (Heb. 12:26-29).

But it won't look secure. It won't look a safe thing to do. To love the word means to be despised by the world. Most of the singer's contemporaries, including no doubt many of those in the official people of God, despise him. Verse 141, 'I am small and despised,' insignificant, a 'child', a nobody in the

The Loyal Love of Goodness (vv. 137-144)

eyes of the world, someone of no status, one who belongs to a fellowship not many of whom were ever rich, mighty, or clever (1 Cor. 1:26), and even if I am rich, mighty or clever, becoming a Christian will cause me to be treated as if I were not; 'yet I do not forget your precepts.' They forget them (v. 139), but I do not forget; I remember, I hear and I obey. And therefore, although the world accounts me small and despised, my future is secure, because, verse 142, 'Your righteousness is righteous for ever', that is, it is as righteous as righteous can be, without limit. 'And your instruction is true', trustworthy. No human activity and no event of history can change it.

So although, verse 143, 'Trouble and anguish have found me out', my life is, in many ways, grim, nevertheless, in the middle of the grimness, 'your commandments are my delight.' I sing, not because this age is comfortable, but because your commandments speak to me of the age to come, in which I will not be small and despised, but I will rule with Christ over the new creation. There is a beauty, a delightfulness, in the word of God, because truth is beautiful. This is the beauty of holiness, not aesthetically pleasing or impressive buildings, but godliness and truth. And so he is learning to delight in goodness. 'Whatever is true, whatever is honourable, whatever is just, whatever is pure, whatever is lovely, whatever is commendable, if there is any excellence, think about these things' (Phil. 4:8). Because these things point the way to life, verse 144, 'Righteous are your testimonies forever; give me understanding, that I may live.'

And so he rejoices in the sheer trustworthiness of the word of God. That the small, despised nobody, who burns with jealous anger for the honour of God, who endures trouble and anguish, may safely rest on this righteous word. Notice that he can affirm the righteous, faithful, true word of God while he is suffering acutely. This means he understands the tenses of the promises, that above all they are promises of future rescue. This understanding is the difference between faith and sight. He can shed tears of present grief all intermingled with tears of future joy.

PERSONAL RESPONSE QUESTIONS

1. What do you know in experience of zeal for God's name, or of being 'small and despised' because you honour his word?

2. How does being despised deepen your delight in the Bible?

19

Section 19:
Prayer and the Promises
(vv. 145-152)

Qoph

[145]I call with my whole heart; answer me, O LORD!
  I will keep your *statutes*.
[146]I call to you; save me,
  that I may observe your *testimonies*.

[147]I wake before dawn and cry for help;
  I hope in your *words*.
[148]They awake, my eyes, before the watches of the night,
  that I may meditate on your *promise*.

[149]Hear my voice according to your steadfast love;
  O LORD, according to your *judgment* give me life.
[150]They draw near who persecute me with evil purpose;
  they are far from your *instruction*.
[151]But you are near, O LORD,
  and all your *commandments* are true.
[152]Long have I known from your *testimonies*
  that you have founded them forever.

The theme of this section is prayer and the promises of God. The first two verses begin with 'I call' (vv. 145, 146). In verse 147, 'I ... cry for help.' In verse 148, 'my eyes' are awake to meditate on the promises. In verse 149 he calls, 'Hear my voice.' In verse 151 he is deeply aware of the nearness of God. Christian experience is urgent prayer shaped by sure promises. The walk of the word is shaped by the promises of the word that call from us heartfelt prayer.

A. PRAYER IS AN URGENT LONGING SHAPED BY SURE PROMISES (VV. 145-148).

Verses 145, 146 are a close pair, each beginning, 'I call'. Verse 145, 'I call with my whole heart' (the whole heart that was commanded in v. 2 and prayed for in v. 10); 'answer me, O LORD! I will keep your statutes', that is, I will keep them when by your grace you answer my call. Verse 146, 'I call to you; save me, that I may observe your testimonies.' This is not, 'I've been a good boy; now you owe me one.' Rather it is, 'I am a believer. The longing of my heart is to keep your word and walk your way. And I can only do that if you answer and save me.' Remember the music of grace throughout the psalm.

The next pair of verses intensify this call. Verse 147, 'I wake before dawn and cry for help; I hope in your words.' There is an urgency here both in the time ('before dawn') and the word 'cry' which suggests an urgent desperate cry for help, such as someone might utter when being attacked or mugged. Verse 148, 'They awake, my eyes, before the watches of the night, that I may meditate on your promise." At both ends of the night and through the night he prays, as Jesus did in Gethsemane: 'Could you not watch with me one hour?' as I cry for help. Real Christian experience is not occasional forays into the world of prayer, but a life shaped by longing for the future, the cry, 'Your kingdom come.' This yearning is so all-consuming it interrupts his sleep. This sleeplessness is not the anxious toil rebuked in Psalm 127:2, but the urgent prayer of the widow commended in Luke 18:1-8. This is the restlessness commended in Isaiah 62:6, 'You who put the

L ORD in remembrance, take no rest, and give him no rest, until he establishes Jerusalem, and makes it a praise in the earth.'

The place of Christian prayer is not the contemplative's armchair but the edge of a hard seat. I do not pray sitting comfortably searching out the presence of God by thinking, meditation, or mysticism. I pray on the edge of a hard seat, longing, craning my neck forward with all creation longing for our adoption as sons, the redemption of our bodies (Rom. 8:18-25).

But it is vital to see that his prayer is shaped by the promises. 'I hope in your words' (v. 147), '... that I may meditate on your promises' (v. 148). He feeds his prayers not with his subjective desires, but with the objective promises. His hope is given shape and substance by the word of God. Although his prayers are first squeezed out of him by the misery of his plight, they take their shape with the wonder of God's promises. So he does not 'listen to God' in a mystical sense, hearing what he thinks God is saying to him, which is so often a sanitised or pious reflection of our own desires. No, he calls on the L ORD to do what he has promised to do in his word. He pleads the promises. He longs not for a future invented by him, but for the destiny promised by God.

And therefore he longs for the kingdom of Christ, for all the promises of God find their 'Yes' in him (2 Cor. 1:20). All the fullness we have in Christ he longs for. We too do not yet see the world ruled by redeemed human beings in justice. But we see Jesus crowned with glory and honour. And we long for the day of his appearing (Heb. 2:6-9).

How important it is, to be clear what he has and has not promised. How many Christians make shipwreck when suffering comes because they think God has broken a promise he never made in the first place. 'It has shaken my faith,' they say. But so often the faith that is shaken is a faith that God has promised me what I would like him to have promised me. I persuade myself that God has promised me healing, or a job, or a marriage, or a child (or a better-behaved child!). And when it doesn't come, I think he has let me down.

I was preaching in the church where I was minister, on the episode in 2 Kings 20 where Hezekiah is ill; and he turns his face to the wall and prays; and Isaiah declares to him that his prayer has been heard and he will live for fifteen more years. At the door a couple who were visiting thanked me warmly for an excellent sermon. My head began to swell as the devil whispered to me that maybe I was really rather a good preacher. But the balloon was quickly punctured when I asked them why they thought it had been so good. They explained that the husband had cancer and they were taking this passage to be the promise of God to *him* of fifteen more years of life. And my heart sank. I had that terrible feeling we preachers so often get, that we have utterly failed. Because God has not promised fifteen more years to that man. I hope he will give him fifteen more years and more, and have mercy on him. But he has not *promised* it in his word. He has not nailed his faithfulness to that promise. And if they think he has, and he dies, what shipwreck will it make of her faith? How hard it will be for his wife if he dies, not only to lose him, which is hard enough, but to think that God has let her down, which is worse still.

We need to let our prayer be shaped, not by our natural desires, but by the promises of the Covenant God. And those promises are so much greater than the little things for which we pray, such as a healing from cancer. Someone may object that that is a very insensitive thing to say, and that mercies don't come much bigger than healings from cancer. But they do. The promises are so much greater that they make even a healing from cancer seem light and trivial by comparison. For the Covenant promise to Abraham's family is that we will inherit the world (Rom. 4:13), that in Christ (who is Abraham's 'seed', Gal. 3:16) the meek inherit the earth (Matt. 5:5). It is for this we need to pray above all, for the keeping of the promises of God. We hope in his words (v. 147) and meditate on his promise (v. 148).

Prayer and the Promises (vv. 145-152)

We must learn the promises, that we may plead the promises. We must study the promises, that they may shape our longings. It follows that the ongoing habits of sitting under biblical preaching and private Bible reading are of great importance.

B. As we pray the promises amidst near enemies, we experience the nearer God (vv. 149-152).

The theme of praying the promises continues in verse 149, 'Hear my voice according to your steadfast (Covenant) love; O LORD, according to your judgment give me life.' The ESV translates, 'According to your justice give me life.' And we have problems with that. We think of the less than beautiful lady being painted by a portrait painter. 'Make sure you do me justice, young man,' she says. And the painter mutters under his breath, 'It is not justice you need, madam, but mercy.' And we think the same of ourselves, that it is not justice we need but mercy, and so we cannot understand how he can pray that in his *justice* God will give him life. But the 'justice' here is the 'judgment', the judicial decision, made by the Covenant God, that all who are justified by faith will have judgment given at the end of time in their favour. They will be vindicated. They cannot finally die.

This is what the Sadducees had failed to understand in Matthew 22. Jesus says that when they read words like, 'I am the God of Abraham and Isaac and Jacob' (Exod. 3:6) they ought to have deduced that there must be a resurrection. No doubt they looked back with puzzled faces and scratched their heads. We do the same. But we too ought to have been able to deduce this, for the logic is quite simple. If I am bound by Covenant to the living God, then that tie cannot be broken. He lives; and therefore I must live. And therefore I cannot die and stay dead. And so the singer prays, 'According to your judgment (your Covenant decision) give me life.' Though I die, yet shall I live (John 11:25).

As he prays this promise for the future, it changes the present. Feel the tension in verses 150, 151. Notice the theme of near and far. Verse 150, 'They draw near who persecute me with evil purpose; they are far from your instruction.' The enemies crowd in. Those who are far from God's instruction will always have in their hearts an intrinsic hostility to those who are near to God's instruction.

This hostility is experienced in many ways. Persecution is not always obvious, outward and identifiable. It encompasses all the pressures that afflict the believer because he is a believer. Those persecutions would include the bereavements, sicknesses and disasters of Job; for although they were not what we would usually call persecution, they came upon him because he was a believer. And Job was not the last believer whom Satan demanded to sift like wheat (Luke 22:31).

As this believer walks in the light, he is surrounded by near darkness. He feels the pressure, the closeness, the threat of the darkness, the claustrophobia of the night. He feels the darkness hemming him in. It invades his workplace, his neighbourhood, his home, his family, even his own thoughts and desires.

Because the world, the flesh, and the devil are far from the instruction of God, they draw near to attack the believer. The believer is in the world, and does not belong to the world, and therefore the world hates him (John 15:19). This nearness of evil is a frightening nearness. And you and I experience it. If we told our stories, some of them would be stories of near evil, crowding in, pressing on us to break us.

But there is another nearness. Verse 151, 'But you are near, O Lord, and all your commandments are true', trustworthy, reliable. I may rest myself on your Covenant word, because your word is true and you are near. I do not always feel your nearness. But I may know it, because it is pledged in your commandments. So we have here both a visible, tangible, nearness of evil, and also an invisible but real substantial nearness of the Covenant God.

Prayer and the Promises (vv. 145-152)

The hymn, 'O Jesus I have promised' captures this double nearness well.

> O let me feel you near me, the world is ever near;
> I see the sights that dazzle, the tempting sounds I hear;
> my foes are ever near me, around me and within;
> but Jesus, draw still nearer and shield my soul from sin!

As in a number of other sections, the eighth verse functions as the climax. Verse 152, 'Long have I known from your testimonies that you have founded them forever.' There is a rock-solid certainty about the word of God that I can rest my destiny on. It has been from all eternity and will be for all ages. No power of hell is able to shake it. And therefore we may confidently pray what they promise; and we may certainly know the nearness of this Covenant God as we are surrounded by the near evil of the world. When the world, the flesh, and the devil draw near, and they crowd around me so that we are stunned by tragedy, numbed by grief, lured by seduction, puffed by flattery, threatened by hostility, or lulled into complacency, we may with confidence draw near to the throne of grace where we find grace to help in time of need (Heb. 4:16). The word of God ties us, and only the word of God, from a painful present to a glorious future.

It follows that sitting regularly under the preaching and encouragement of the word of God is enormously important. Sometimes when Christians move house they do not consider where they are going to belong to a church in which the word of God is faithfully preached. They think they can be loners, or like camels, with riches stored up from their last church. 'I've heard the word of God once. That's all I need. I'll be alright for the next 30 years.' It doesn't work like that. I need the regular nearness of the word of God to bring home to my heart the nearness of the God of the word. And I need it because I am surrounded by near evil.

Bible Delight

1. Are there times when you are more conscious of the nearness of evil than of the closeness of the LORD? How can this section help?

2. How can you make sure that you pray for what is promised, and not just for what you want?

20

Section 20:
The Trustworthy Word
(vv. 153-160)

Resh

¹⁵³Look on my affliction and deliver me,
  for I do not forget your *instruction*.
¹⁵⁴Plead my cause and redeem me;
  give me life according to your *promise*!

¹⁵⁵Salvation is far from the wicked,
  for they do not seek your *statutes*.
¹⁵⁶Great is your mercy, O LORD;
  give me life according to your *judgments*.

¹⁵⁷Great are my persecutors and my adversaries,
  but I do not swerve from your *testimonies*.
¹⁵⁸I look at the faithless with disgust,
  because they do not keep your *promises*.
¹⁵⁹Consider how I love your *precepts*!
  Give me life according to your steadfast love.

¹⁶⁰The sum of your *word* is truth,
  and every one of your righteous *judgments* endures forever.

THE COVENANT GOD NEVER CHANGES HIS MIND.

Section 20 is quite similar to Section 19. They are tied by the climactic final verses, verse 152 about the sureness of the word, and verse 160 pressing home the same point. Each section ends with the word 'forever'.

Verse 153, 'Look on my affliction and deliver me, for I do not forget your instruction.' We met this affliction in verses 50, 67, 71, 75, and it has not stopped. This was the affliction that proved to him that he did not belong in this age. It was a blessing for it drove him to walk in the way of the word. This affliction was like an electric fence to a sheep, painful but necessary to keep him safe.

Verse 154, 'Plead my cause' (literally, plead my pleading in court, be my Advocate) 'and redeem me; give me life according to your promise!' Again, as in verse 122 he prays for the Cross, though he does not know it.

Verse 155, 'Salvation is far from the wicked, for they do not seek your statutes.' The righteous by faith are not the only people needing rescue. Every human being longs for rescue, from frustration, from mortality, from disappointment, from pain, from the experience that 'to all all-ness I see a cutting off' (v. 96). But if they are 'far from your instruction' (v. 150), then they are far from you and therefore far from rescue. They long for rescue. But their longings will be frustrated. That is not true for the believer. Every morning the believer can wake up and say 'today salvation is nearer to me now than when I first believed' (Rom. 13:11). And that is a marvellous truth. You have a rubbish Monday? You can wake on Tuesday morning and say 'Salvation is nearer to me than when I first believed.' You have a bad Tuesday? You can wake on Wednesday morning and say the same!

Some years ago I was speaking to a man who attended church. He was about forty years old and struggling in a difficult marriage. I said to him, 'Hang on in there with faithfulness; it is only another thirty or forty years.' Although that may sound silly, I was serious.

The Trustworthy Word (vv. 153-160)

Sadly, I think he thought I was joking; that length of time felt like eternity to him, and he did not hang on in there. But actually that is a Christian attitude, to think that thirty or forty years may feel a very long time; but in the perspective of eternity it isn't.

Then in verses 156, 157 there is a contrast of two big things. In the last section there was a contrast of nearness. Now there is a contrast of bigness. Verse 156: 'Great is your mercy, O Lord; give me life according to your judgments.' He rejoices in a great mercy, the movement of God's kidneys (as it were) in compassion, the movement of the emotions that turned the Lord Jesus inside out when he felt such a gut-wrenching compassion for the lost as he saw them like sheep without a shepherd (Matt. 9:36). The Lord's heart overflows with mercy; this is how he feels towards you and me.

The believer needs this great mercy because he is surrounded by great enemies. Verse 157: 'Great (i.e. many, the same word) are my persecutors and my adversaries, but I do not swerve from your testimonies.'

The old hymn puts this double greatness well, when it says,

> He gives us more grace when the burdens grow greater,
> he sends us more strength when the labours increase;
> to greater affliction he adds his great mercy,
> to multiplied trials, his multiplied peace.

What is Christian experience? Great enemies, but a greater mercy. Near enemies, but a nearer God. And so he is afflicted, but not crushed (2 Cor. 4:8).

His loyalty surfaces again in verse 158 : 'I look at the faithless' (those who break faith with God, who don't keep Covenant) 'with disgust because they do not keep your promises.' This is a mark of his passionate loyalty to the Lord. When he looks at those who break faith with this faithful God, he cannot help being appalled, including, no doubt, at his own past. How could they (how could I?) not be loyal to such a loyal God? How could we break faith with such a faithful God?

This disgust is the necessary companion of the love of verse 159: 'Consider how I love your precepts! Give me life according to your steadfast love' (an echo of v. 149). He does not always do the thing he loves to do, but in his heart of hearts there is a love for the precepts of God, because God has written this word on his heart.

And then again, as in Section 19, the final verse is the climax, signalled partly by having two of the regular eight 'word' words squeezed into it. Verse 160, 'The sum of your word is truth, and every one of your righteous judgments endures forever.' The 'sum' means something like 'head, source, beginning' of God's word. So this verse speaks of a word that was true from a past eternity and will be true forever in the future.

Every judgment, every decision, of God lasts for ever. Or, to put it another way, no decision of God will be overturned on appeal. This is a wonderful truth. Satan is a lawyer who is a habitual appealer against the judgments of God. So he comes to God with a bulging briefcase and says, 'Lord, I know you have given judgment in favour of so-and-so. I know you have declared them justified by faith. You have announced now your verdict in the final judgment, that they are justified and will not be condemned. But, if you will forgive my saying so, I do not think that was a good decision, because he is a rubbish person. And here is my evidence.' And out of his bulging briefcase he gets an enormous bundle of closely-typed papers, listing in detail every sin of thought, word and deed, committed by the person in question. And it is all true. 'So will you not reconsider your verdict, your judgment?' And the Lord brushes him aside and waves him away. 'No,' he says, 'this man or woman is in Christ. I have decided they are justified. And every one of my righteous judgments endures forever.'

From beginning of creation to the end of time, from time immemorial to time without end, his Covenant word is true and reliable. It is this sure word, and only this word, that ties us from a painful present to a glorious future. We are not tied to the future by our natural longings or desires, or by our pain, but by his written promises in Christ. This is Christian experience.

So the authentic Christian answer to the question, 'How are you?' is, 'I am holding on. I am held by the Covenant promises of God in Christ. I am surrounded by near enemies and great enemies. I feel the darkness around and within. And yet I know from the word a nearer God and a greater mercy. And I rest my present and my future on this word that is true from the dawn of time and will remain true to all eternity.'

PERSONAL RESPONSE QUESTIONS

1. How does this section help you rest your confidence on the word of God as the only sure anchor in a dangerous world?

2. Are you more aware of the greatness of your problems and spiritual foes, or of the greatness of the LORD's mercy? How can you get these in the right balance?

21

Section 21:
The Future
Brought into the Present
(vv. 161-168)

Sin and Shin

[161]Princes persecute me without cause,
   but to your *words* my heart stands in awe.
[162]I rejoice at your *promise*
   like one who finds great spoil.

[163]I hate and abhor falsehood,
   but I love your *instruction*.
[164]Seven times a day I praise you
   for your righteous *judgments*.

[165]Great peace have those who love your *instruction*;
   nothing can make them stumble.
[166]I hope for your salvation, O LORD,
   and I do your *commandments*.
[167]My soul keeps your *testimonies*;
   I love them deeply.
[168]I keep your *precepts* and *testimonies*,
   for all my ways are before you.

THE WORD OF GOD BRINGS THE EXPERIENCE OF THE
FUTURE INTO THE PRESENT.

The theme of this penultimate section is that only the word of
God brings a foretaste of the future into present Christian experience. We have seen that the word of God ties us from a painful
present to a glorious future. But this is stronger; for a foretaste
of that future is actually brought into present experience.

This builds on the double climax from the eighth verse of
the last two sections. Verse 152, 'Long have I known from your
testimonies that you have founded them forever.' Verse 160,
'The sum of your word is truth, and every one of your righteous
judgments endures forever.' This double climax sends our singer
up to the most upbeat of all the stanzas. If Section 11 was the
midnight of the psalm, this is the noonday. 'How are you?' 'I'm
good! I'm great, thanks.' This section is trumpets all the way.

His situation has not changed. Verse 161, 'Princes persecute
me without cause', just as they have been doing ever since
verse 23. As David was pursued by Saul, and as the Lord Jesus
was persecuted by his enemies, so this believer knows what it is
to be treated unfairly by powerful people, to be zealous, and yet
to suffer, for doing good (1 Pet. 3:13, 17).

But although powerful people persecute him, he is not in awe
of them, as we might expect him to be. I find myself naturally
in awe of powerful people, and potent human symbols. I have
only to emerge from the Underground or Metro into the
central business district of a great banking city like London to
find myself wanting to bow down and worship in awe before
the great god Mammon. But this believer's response is different.
'Princes persecute me without cause, but to your words my heart
stands in awe' ('to your words' is emphatic in the Hebrew). He
does not fear the one who can kill the body but cannot kill
the soul; but he stands in awe of the one who casts soul and
body into hell. Like the Christian wife oppressed by an ungodly
husband, she does not give way to fear (1 Pet. 3:6), because she
too stands in awe of God's words.

The Future Brought into the Present (vv. 161-168)

And in the presence of these awesome words, a great catena or chain of future grace is brought into his present experience, as he is overwhelmed by joy, love, praise, peace, and hope.

First, in verse 162 he finds joy. 'I rejoice at your promise like one who finds great spoil.' This word joins him like an anchor to the harbour in the midst of a storm-tossed sea. Spoil is, as Calvin says, thrice welcome. For it is found at a time of victory; it is of great value; and it is unexpected. I thought I was a loser, and the world thinks I am a loser, but I find in the word of God that I am a winner; God is for me. I thought I was poor and find in the word that I am rich, with all the fullness of Christ. I thought it was just tough tough tough, and unexpectedly I stumble on the pearl of great price. I find that as one of Abraham's family, Christ's family, I am heir of the world; I will inherit the earth; the world is mine, all things are mine in Christ. And so even as princes persecute me, I rejoice.

This joy is a challenge to us. For whatever we may say in theory about the Bible in our doctrinal statements, until we rejoice in it we are practical liberals. Our joy in the word is the litmus test of the value we actually place on that word.

Second, in the presence of these awesome words, he finds love. Love is one of the hallmarks of this section. It comes three times, in verse 163, verse 165, and verse 167. Verse 163, 'I hate and abhor falsehood, but I love your instruction.' My value system is turned inside out by the word of God. I had disordered love, loving what I ought to hate and hating what I ought to love. But the word of God is setting my loves in order.

Third, in the presence of these awesome words he finds praise. Verse 164, 'Seven times a day I praise you for your righteous judgments.' The expression 'seven times a day' is a poetic way of describing a life filled in every part with praise (cf. Ps. 55:17, 'Evening and morning and noon'; or Dan. 6:10). He gets on with all the normal chores and business of life; he does the washing-up and the ironing. He is not an impractical mystic. But in it all, his life is shot through with praise. Whatever is worthy of praise, he praises. And supremely he praises the God of his salvation. And he does this in the midst of suffering. For the princes still persecute him.

One of William Wilberforce's friends paid him a beautiful tribute. After listing his talents, he wrote, 'Above all, his friends will never cease to remember that peculiar sunshine which he threw over a company by the influence of a mind perpetually turned to *love* and *praise* …. As he walked about the house he was generally humming the tune of a hymn or psalm as if he could not contain his pleasurable feelings of thankfulness and devotion.' Wilberforce knew struggles and controversies. He knew about princes persecuting him. But he was full of praise. I wonder if our friends could say that about us. I fear that all too often under pressure I moan and grumble about the house like a perpetual Eeyore.

Fourth, in the presence of this awesome word he finds peace. Verse 165, 'Great peace have those who love your instruction; nothing can make them stumble.' He knows a great peace, a rich peace, a deep peace. No pitfalls can trap him as he walks the way. The world, the flesh and the devil will do their wicked best to make him stumble, by pride, lust, gluttony, complacency, covetousness, unforgiveness, resentment, or anxiety. In a thousand ways they try to trip him. But for one who loves his instruction there is great peace. He can walk in the light in the midst of darkness, because God's word is a lamp to his path.

Fifth, in the presence of this awesome word he finds hope. Verse 166, 'I hope for your salvation, O Lord, and I do your commandments.' The word of God brings the future into the present, because it ties us by a sure and certain hope to the age to come. It is the aroma of a banquet sensed in the air before the dining doors open. I hope, and hope does not disappoint, hope will not end in shame, because the love of God has been poured into our hearts by his Spirit (Rom. 5:5). Sometimes as we hear the word of God we will be deeply moved as hope stirs afresh in our hearts.

The Future Brought into the Present (vv. 161-168)

Then, in verse 167, as in verse 163, there is love again. 'My souls keeps your testimonies; I love them exceedingly.' Notice how the intensity of this future grace is conveyed by words and expressions like 'exceedingly' (v. 167), 'awe' (v. 161), 'seven times a day' (v. 164), and 'great' (v. 165).

Again, the eighth verse is climactic. Verse 168, 'I keep your precepts and testimonies, for all my ways are before you.' Notice that two of the regular eight 'word' words appear here for emphasis (as in two other final verses of sections, v. 48 and v. 160). Near where I live there were advertisements recently appealing to me to buy a Kit-Kat so that I may 'win a chance to be a housemate,' that is, to enter the 'Big Brother' house. Personally I can think of little worse and am avoiding Kit-Kats for the present and sticking with Twix; I suggest you do the same. The prospect of 'all my ways' being open to millions of critical viewers all voting to have me expelled is not an appealing one.

How much worse, we might think, for 'all my ways' to be open to the God who sees the heart. Like a spider scuttling for cover from the light, by nature we love darkness rather than light (John 3:19). And yet he can sing with joy, 'for all my ways are before you'. My life is an open book. The way I take, the walk I walk, the talk I talk, it is open before you. He can live life cheerfully *coram Deo* (in the presence of God). How is this possible? Because of the Covenant, which points forward to the promises fulfilled in Christ. The Covenant only makes sense because of the Cross. Because the Covenant God is 'for' him (Rom. 8:31), because he has pledged to give judgment in his favour, because of the sacrifice of Christ, therefore he knows that as a believer he can walk with joy, love, praise, peace, hope and boldness in the presence of God. It is a great upbeat section, this number 21 out of 22. But why doesn't he finish on this one? That is the question we have to ask when we study number 22.

Bible Delight

1. What experience do you have of joy, love, praise, peace, hope and boldness before God in the midst of pressure?

2. How can this section lead you into more of these experiences?

22

Section 22:
Unresolved Tension
Dependent on Grace
(vv. 169-176)

Taw

[169]Let my cry draw near before you, O Lord;
   give me understanding according to your *word*!
[170]Let my plea come before you;
   deliver me according to your *promise*.

[171]My lips will pour forth praise,
   for you teach me your *statutes*.
[172]My tongue will sing of your *promise*,
   for all your *commandments* are right.

[173]Let your hand be ready to help me,
   for I have chosen your *precepts*.
[174]I long for your salvation, O Lord,
   and your *instruction* is my delight.

[175]Let my soul live and praise you,
   and let your *judgments* help me.
[176]I have gone astray like a lost sheep;
   seek your servant,
      for I do not forget your *commandments*.

AUTHENTIC CHRISTIAN EXPERIENCE IS UNRESOLVED TENSION DEPENDENT UPON GRACE.

The theme of this puzzling final section is that present Christian experience is unresolved tension dependent upon grace.

How do you end a great psalm like this? Part of me almost wishes he had left it unfinished. Then we could have had a competition, as one might do with Dickens' final and unfinished novel, *The Mystery of Edwin Drood*, which he was writing when he died. The start was crisp and powerful: three verses of crystal truth and then five verses of heartfelt response. The second last section was strong. But on the face of it our singer does not finish well. It does seem a poor ending.

For myself, I would have ended something like this. 'Listen to me! I am a great Bible scholar. I have written an amazing 22-Section 8-verse per section acrostic about the word of God. It is intricately structured and theologically profound. And I want you to know that although I have had my struggles, I am now living the victorious Christian life. I want you to know this so you will invite me to your conferences and put on your brochures photographs of me with perfect teeth, a pretty wife, a fast car, a large office, and an aura of success and prosperity. I want you saying of me, "This man is a success, in his discipleship, in his marriage, in his family, in his ministry." ' That is how I would end, to go out on a high.

But it's such an odd last section. To the shallow observer it looks as if the psalm was 95% inspired, but then on the last section the inspiration ran out. Musically it is so odd, because it keeps switching key. It begins in a minor key with a pair of prayer verses: verse 169, 'Let my cry come before you, O LORD' – oh, no! we're back to crying again; I thought we had got beyond prayer and into praise – 'give me understanding according to your promise!' that is, change me from the inside, give me wisdom, understanding in the inner person. (To be given understanding means more than to be given cognitive content; it means to be changed inside.) Verse 170, 'Let my plea come before you; deliver me according to your word,' that is, give me understanding, change me from the inside, and then cause me to persevere to the end that I may be rescued, as you have promised ('according to your promise'). We are back to desperate prayer, where we have been so often before. Have we made no progress? It doesn't seem so.

But then he shifts into a major key, (an emphatically major key) for the next pair. Verse 171, 'My lips will pour forth praise,' literally, let them bubble up with praise, let me be like a fresh-water spring. This is loud and exuberant. Just as the created order pours forth speech in the poetry of Psalm 19:2 (using the same word), so the believer pours forth praise. Why such praise? '... for you teach me your statutes.' Half a dozen times he has prayed, 'Teach me your statutes,' that is, teach me to do them. And God is answering his prayer! He bubbles up with praise when he realizes that the God who made the Andromeda Galaxy is at work in his heart changing him. He is learning to walk the walk.

As the converted slave-trader John Newton once put it,

I am not what I ought to be;
I am not what I wish to be;
I am not what I hope to be;
But by the grace of God I am not what I was.

This power to change him from the inside by the Covenant word makes him bubble up with praise. What a wonderful God. It is a similar feeling of wonder to that which John the Baptist had when he spoke of the one coming after him. 'I can baptise you with water', he said. That is, 'I can do the outside religious stuff. I can preach. I can make your skin wet as the outward sign of inner cleansing. But I cannot change your heart. And yet after me comes the one who can. He will do what no human being before or since can do: he will baptise you with the Holy Spirit. He will teach you his statutes. He will write his law in your heart so that you walk in them. He will change you on the inside. He will give you new birth.' What a wonderful Saviour!

Churches where men and women are being changed by the word and Spirit of God ought to be marked by a praise that puts others in the shade. This praise should bubble up out of changed lives. And it continues in verse 172, 'My tongue will sing of your promise, for all your commandments are right.' They are good; they are true; they are life-changing.

But then, just when we thought he was going to end well, we go back into a minor key. Verse 173, 'Let your hand (the hand of rescue, cf. Deut. 4:34) be ready to help me, for I have chosen your precepts.' Again, a desperate urgent plea for rescue. We do not seem to have reached 'the victorious Christian life'! Verse 174, 'I long for your salvation, O Lord,' – and then, mid verse, back into major key, 'and your law is my delight.' Verse 175, 'Let my soul live and praise you,' – and then back into petition – 'and let your judgments help me.' He cannot make up his mind whether he is in prayer or praise. Because that is how it is in authentic Christian experience.

This tension is highlighted by the final verse of the psalm, which is in some ways the oddest verse of all. Certainly it will be deleted from the Bible by the shallow triumphalist. Verse 176, 'I have gone astray like a lost sheep.' We won't want to invite him to our conference platform. The verb 'go astray' is used in Psalm 95:10 of the disobedient people of Israel in the wilderness, and in Psalm 58:3 of the wicked. It is not impressive to include himself among their number. This is, incidentally, the proof that verses like verse 67 ('Before I was afflicted I went astray, but now I keep your promise') are not claims to sinless perfection.

Spare a thought for the Goldsborough 2nd XI cricket team. In July 2006 there was a cricket match in the Nidderdale and District Amateur Cricket League in North Yorkshire. Dishforth beat Goldsborough 2nd XI. Goldsborough had a disappointing day. Their first batsman was out for a duck; and the second; and the third; and the 4th, 5th, 6th, 7th, 8th, 9th, and 10th. And the 11th man was 'nought, not out'. They did score a leg-bye and four byes, so there were 5 runs on the board. But you would have to say they need help.

How disappointing that the writer of this psalm places himself with Goldsborough 2nd XI rather than with a Test Cricket team. He does not finish well. We do not think that God wants failures like that on his team. But gloriously, he does! Who is this great believer, who has written this wonderful psalm? Answer: a lost sheep!

In the Christian world we love to follow heroes. But we do not always choose them well. I remember receiving through the post a brochure about a conference. All the speakers were handsome or beautiful and looked successful. Against one of them the blurb said that this man had 'coached 100,000 pastors into transitioning into growth.' And I thought, 'Wow! I wish I could be as successful as that.' Then I would have no need of the grace of God; I could stand on my own, and people could praise me. And then I thought, 'They would never have had the Apostle Paul on their platform. They would never have had the writer of Psalm 119. And they would never have had the Lord Jesus. We love to say of someone in church life, 'Isn't Fred(a) amazing?' But Fred(a) is not amazing. He or she is a lost sheep.

Our singer is so deeply aware of his weakness, as he continues, 'seek your servant, for I do not forget your commandments.' That is, he affirms that he is a believer; that he does not forget the commandments is an evidence of grace. And one of the marks of the real believer is a strong awareness of frailty, and reliance upon grace. 'I have gone astray.' That's what I do by nature. In my flesh there dwells no good thing (Rom. 7:18). I will always go astray unless you seek me. I will never seek you unless you first seek me.

Without the hand of the Good Shepherd watching me moment by moment I will always go astray. If you leave me unwatched for a nanosecond, I will leave the path. And I will not come back by nature. Sometimes we think that as believers our wanderings are not so much the wanderings of sheep as the wandering of a pet dog. We have a very dim dog at home. But he is not as dim as a sheep. Sometimes it is a close call; but although he will run off and chase a squirrel or a rabbit, he will come back in the end (so far, at least). We think that now we are Christians, yes, we will wander, but we will naturally find our way home given time. So you don't need to worry about us. But we won't. By nature we are still sheep, and we will go astray, and we will never return home unless the Shepherd seeks us. And it is only by the constant watchful seeking of God as he watches over us by his Spirit, that we are kept on the path.

You and I can go out of an inspiring Christian meeting, our thoughts full of the wonder of God. And within seconds we can find ourselves snapping bad temperedly at a member of our family, lusting after someone who is not our spouse, turning over covetous thoughts in our minds. It never ceases to astonish me how quickly it happens. But I ought not to be astonished; I ought not to be in the least surprised. Calvin comments that, 'such is our liability to err, that we immediately relapse into sin the instant he leaves us to ourselves.'

If verse 176 takes us by surprise, it is because we have slipped back into getting the tone of voice wrong. We have forgotten the music of grace. We have begun to sing in a tone not of penitence but boasting, not of dependence upon grace but of self-righteousness, not of strength made perfect in weakness but of strength expressed in confident victory. This last verse is a forceful reminder that the music of the psalm is the music of grace.

This final section may be disappointing. But it is so realistic. 'How are you?' 'I don't know. I feel in a complete muddle. I don't know whether I am up or down. I long with passionate desperate longing for the salvation of God. I am full of pleading and prayer and yearning. And at the same time the promise of God fills me with joy, praise, peace, love and hope. I am all tensions. And I cast myself on the grace of God and the word of God.'

And as so often in the Bible, the end of the psalm is not the end of the story. If we think of the psalm as portraying the believer as a building under construction, this last verse is a reminder that the scaffolding is still in place. At the end of this psalm we are still in painful tension. This is how it is. This psalm will not be sung in the age to come. But for now it is authentic Christian experience. This is so realistic.

'How are you?' 'I really don't know. I cannot work out whether I am in prayer or praise. I seem to feel both strongly and inconsistently.' That is the authentic Christian response. There are two simpler responses; and neither of them is Christian. If I just say it is grim grim grim, that is not an authentic Christian response. And if I say it is great great great that also is not an authentic Christian response. The authentic response is to say I really don't know. I am held by the word of God from a painful present to a glorious future. And that word brings into the present a foretaste of joy, hope, peace and praise. And the praise is all muddled up with the prayer. I don't know whether to laugh or cry; and I do both at the same time. That is authentic Christian experience. This is why it is so easy for the Christian church to slip to one side or the other, into a shallow triumphalism or just into gloom.

The people of God delight in the word of God, because this word alone ties us in the pain of the present to the glory of the future. May God help us to sing it.

PERSONAL RESPONSE QUESTIONS

1. Does your experience match the tensions in this last section?

2. How does it help us to live with both urgent prayer and heart-felt praise at the same time?

Conclusion:
Bible Delight

I want in conclusion to commend this psalm as a nourishing ingredient in the spiritual diet of the preacher and Bible teacher. Our preaching and teaching will always tend to revert from a heart of Bible delight towards a hard and cold heart of Bible duty. Our right concern for truth will always by nature be tending to move away from truth on fire and towards ossified orthodoxy. By meditating on this psalm we put ourselves alongside a fellow Bible teacher whose preaching is indeed truth on fire, because it stems from a heart on fire with love for the LORD expressed in love for his word.

As we make his words our words, our hearts too will be rekindled. They will be set on fire by the steady faithfulness of the Covenant God fulfilled in Jesus Christ. They will be fired afresh by the steadfast love of the Covenant God who promises rescue to all who are in Covenant relation with him through faith in Jesus Christ. They will be warmed by the delights of his pledged and promised love in the treasures of his word.

And as our hearts are warmed and rekindled, so we may pray that the hearts of our hearers will likewise be softened, their ears and eyes opened, and their spirits revived by this same steady Covenant word in Christ.

Oh, how I love your instruction!
All the day it is my meditation.

(Ps. 119:97)

Note about Commentaries

Easily the most profitable part of my study has been translating and meditating on the psalm verse by verse in the original Hebrew. Most commentaries are much too brief to be helpful with the detail of this psalm. This includes Kidner, whose comments are always insightful; there are just too few of them. L. C. Allen is accurate and useful in the Word Biblical Commentary series, but again very brief. The exception is Calvin, whose commentary is full, theologically perceptive and pastorally sensitive. I mined Spurgeon for some happy ways of expressing devotional truths. Marcus Nodder wrote an accurate and observant analysis of the structures of the psalm in *Churchman*, which confirmed to me that the psalm is the product of a deeply ordered mind, and drew my attention to some features of structure I had not noticed in my own translation.

About the Proclamation Trust

The Proclamation Trust is all about unashamedly preaching and teaching God's Word, the Bible. Our firm conviction is that when God's Word is taught, God's voice is heard, and therefore our entire work is about helping people engage in this life-transforming work.

We have three strands to our ministry:

Firstly we run the Cornhill Training Course which is a three-year, part-time course to train people to handle and communicate God's Word rightly.

Secondly we have a wide portfolio of conferences we run to equip, enthuse and energise senior pastors, assistant pastors, students, ministry wives, women in ministry and church members in the work God has called them to. We also run the Evangelical Ministry Assembly each summer in London which is a gathering of over a thousand church leaders from across the UK and from around the world.

Thirdly we produce an array of resources, of which this book in your hand is one, to assist people in preaching, teaching and understanding the Bible.

For more information please go to www.proctrust.org.uk

ISBN 978-1-84550-347-5

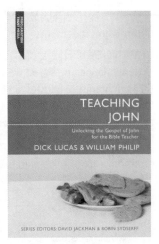

ISBN 978-1-85792-790-0

ISBN 978-1-84550-255-3

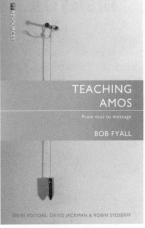

ISBN 978-1-84550-142-6

Christian Focus Publications

Our mission statement —

STAYING FAITHFUL

In dependence upon God we seek to impact the world through literature faithful to His infallible Word, the Bible. Our aim is to ensure that the Lord Jesus Christ is presented as the only hope to obtain forgiveness of sin, live a useful life and look forward to heaven with Him.

Our books are published in four imprints:

CHRISTIAN
FOCUS

Popular works including biographies, commentaries, basic doctrine and Christian living.

CHRISTIAN
HERITAGE

Books representing some of the best material from the rich heritage of the church.

MENTOR

Books written at a level suitable for Bible College and seminary students, pastors, and other serious readers. The imprint includes commentaries, doctrinal studies, examination of current issues and church history.

CF4•K

Children's books for quality Bible teaching and for all age groups: Sunday school curriculum, puzzle and activity books; personal and family devotional titles, biographies and inspirational stories — because you are never too young to know Jesus!

Christian Focus Publications Ltd,
Geanies House, Fearn, Ross-shire,
IV20 1TW, Scotland, United Kingdom.
www.christianfocus.com